CRA[illegible]NG CULTURE

How to make employment happier and achieve exceptional business success

PAULA MITCHELL

Enquiries: paula@thecondorcollective.com

Book design by Helen Nelson, www.jetthedog.co.uk

Edited by Ilsa Hawtin, www.wordsure.co.uk

ISBN: 978-1-7384883-0-8

Some names and characteristics have been changed to protect the privacy of the individuals involved.

For Anna and Teddy,
employees or entrepreneurs of the future

CONTENTS

PREFACE

It probably should have dawned on me earlier. It was what my whole career was based around, after all … but sometimes the dots connect when you least expect. One night in 2013, at a works event on the banks of the Thames, I realised there was something fundamentally wrong with employment.

I'd been working for a few years in the male-dominated sphere of construction recruitment. My customers were great fun – full of the brass authenticity that gives the construction industry its wonderfully unaffected reputation. I'd learned to laugh off generally inoffensive judgements about my own line of work, but there was something that suddenly rankled with me when I overheard a conversation that evening.

I was ensconced amongst a cheery group of cockney charmers and cuddly beer bellies when I earwigged a conversation behind me.

'Who's that woman talking to Mark?' one of the guys asked.
'It's Paula. She's a recruitment consultant.'
'Bloody recruitment consultants – they get everywhere. Wish they'd piss off from these sorts of things.'

This kind of comment was nothing new. There are more complimentary things said about politicians than recruiters, which isn't a contest where you want to come second.

Fear not – this doesn't continue as a sob story for recruitment consultants. There's something much more important to deal with than that. That evening, against the auspicious backdrop of the London skyline, after listening to yet another condemnation of my career choice, I realised two things.

1. There was something missing in my own work. I wasn't sure why I was doing the job I was doing anymore, and growing a business was taking its toll.

2. I realised I spent every day at work talking to other people who were unhappy in their jobs. And that was a lot of people.

Both of these points – especially the second – led me to change the path of my career.

As a recruitment consultant, I was in constant contact with employees who were everything from apathetic about their jobs to downright miserable about the whole world of employment. They'd talk about micromanagement, bullying tactics, unpaid overtime, poor communication, stifling bureaucracy, poor recognition and lack of direction, not to mention being slow clapped out of the office if they ever left work on time. The leaders were unhappy too. The pressure to keep the business afloat and to inspire and motivate an often entitled team, all the while feeling unappreciated and overworked, tarnished their experience too. There were some moments of happiness in there, but they were too frequently buried within the cesspit of negativity.

As I viewed the stunning London skyline from the pod on the Eye, I zoned out from the raucous laughter around me, one question ringing clear in my mind:

Shouldn't employment be happier?

This instigated a quest to create happier employment.

We are a single race of humans, who thrive on each other's companionship, guidance, fun and care, yet we seem to have turned the workplace into a test of endurance, where we struggle to exhibit some of our most innate human qualities.

My work and research in this area have made it clear to me that happier employment can be realised only as a result of deliberate actions by members of all levels within an organisation.

This book is not directed only at leaders and managers. This book is directed at every single person in any organisation. The drive and ability to improve things does not come with authority. The power to create happier employment is available to all of us.

INTRODUCTION

According to Gallup's 2023 report 'State of the Global Workplace', only 23% of employees worldwide actually like their jobs. That leaves 77% enduring their work rather than enjoying it. The statistics for engagement in the UK provide bleaker reading: 10% engagement, 76% not engaged, and 14% actively disengaged. Eugh.

Thankfully, the data gathered by The Condor Collective, the business I cofounded in 2019, paints a brighter picture. However, we only need ask a group of friends how they feel about their work to be met with responses expressing disdain, apathy or contempt.

While there are many parts of employment that people enjoy, few organisations (and employees) prioritise happiness. There's no metric for it in most companies, yet there is an endless supply of research demonstrating that happier employees perform far better than miserable ones.

Happiness is probably the only thing that every single person on the planet genuinely wants. However, for the vast majority of the world, happiness in the workplace is something of legend – a kind of personal El Dorado. Often people don't know what makes them happy, and happiness is pursued incrementally, more often than not feeling out of reach.

Employees, leaders included, seem to have accepted that happiness is something we need to find outside of work – that it's natural to have to counterbalance the misery of the workplace with the happiness we gain in our free time. This is simply not good enough. While taking care of our mental wellbeing is increasingly encouraged within our everyday lives, it's amazing we have such low expectations during the majority of our working hours.

What creates happiness is, of course, subjective. That makes it tricky – and wonderfully challenging – to get it right for everyone, or at least for the majority of employees. But evidence shows that in so much of our organisational culture, ideology and strategy, creating happiness is rarely discussed as an objective. Even those organisations that recognise the importance of workplace happiness can misconceive its complexity. Buying a new coffee machine, creating a dojo boardroom or publicising a wellbeing strategy on a website are well-meant intentions, but I doubt leaders would strategise achieving sales or product objectives with a snappy message, free doughnuts and fruit bowls.

To improve happiness at work, we need to treat it in the same way as we treat other essential business objectives.

Most of us feel pleasure in making other people happy and in getting along with people. But at work we are conditioned to cultures and practices that can actively deprive us of happiness. These include hierarchical structures, power and ego, subjectivity and bias, tactless communication, irrational behaviour and negativity, not to mention hiring practices that fail to match people to jobs effectively in the first place.

Research has thankfully developed into the field of positive psychology over the last 30 years, focusing on what contributes to our happiness. Before this, all psychology research and practice focused on how to help those who are profoundly unhappy. Leaders and employees are taught little about psychology at school or in the workplace. It's therefore no wonder we struggle to understand each other when most of us have barely learned to understand ourselves. Decades of research confirms that happiness positively affects performance; reduces absenteeism and turnover; and benefits customer satisfaction, innovation, and ultimately revenue. Yet happiness is still considered too fluffy, woo woo and abstract for serious consideration by most organisations.

Leaders hold a significant role in determining employees' happiness, from influencing the organisation's culture to developing engagement strategies. While most books on this subject orientate to the onus of workplace happiness being the leaders' responsibility, this book seeks to offer a perspective on the bilateral and interdependent relationship and on the responsibilities of employers and employees to create a happier workplace.

Employees are *equally* responsible for their leaders' happiness as leaders are for the happiness of employees.

From childhood we are conditioned to an authoritarian construct: the building blocks of our lives are put in place by parents and teachers from whom we learn and receive praise. Within this construct, we don't typically learn to look up and thank those people or give praise in return. This feeling is compounded in the workplace, where employees rarely think about how to help create the best opportunity for happiness for their leaders – or for their peers, for that matter. Organisations, especially larger ones, are often seen as depersonalised entities rather than collections of real people. This book will show how vital it is to recognise that every person in the workplace has similar motivational needs.

Rather than augmenting any 'them and us' culture in the workplace, this book strives to achieve the exact opposite. Creating unity is about understanding. By considering both employers' and employees' perspectives, and challenging our beliefs, behaviour and practices, we can establish a new era of happier employment.

Chapter 1 of this book explores an understanding of happiness itself, the value of work, and why and how things need to change. The remaining chapters challenge our thoughts and beliefs about employment happiness and the thoughts and beliefs we have about ourselves, about others and about work. You will also find a number of pointers to stop and think, and practical tips you can use to shape your culture, behaviour and practices. Each chapter can sit in isolation from the others, so if you find yourself less interested in a particular chapter's content, then whizz on to the next one. Reading is wonderful for inspiration and information, but we don't commit everything we read to memory. I encourage you to choose the most interesting topics and tips for you, and commit to using them and telling other people about them. This is how you will create happier employment.

Using my experience as an entrepreneur and my many years listening to employee and leader experiences, I have distilled the vital information and put it into a context and language that other organisational leaders and employees will recognise. This book is an easily digestible overview of workplace psychology, ideas and practices, specifically created to help you improve your employment experience. I don't profess to be a moral authority on behaviour or employment – I'm a work in progress too. In fact, the stories herein are cathartic confessions of sorts. I hope my failings may encourage you to forgive your own, and to accept that the only way is up if you are willing to recognise your behaviours and invest the effort to do better. I will help you change the way you look at employment and happiness, and to move forward into a hopeful, expectant, happier era of employment.

We might not suddenly find ourselves skipping our way to work, opening our laptops with heady excitement and inviting our managers to dinner twice a month. But we can do better. We need to change the answer to the question How's work? Because just okay is not okay.

HOW SHOULD I KNOW?

While at university and still pondering future opportunities, I signed up for the Jiig Cal computer programme supplied by the university's careers service. I spent 30 minutes entering my personal data, experience and qualifications. I then clearly remember sitting in anticipation, tapping my fingernails on the desk, as I waited for the spinning wheel to stop and my new direction in life to appear …

Prison officer

Music teacher

Fish farm manager

What on Earth? I didn't remember expressing a specific interest in fish anywhere in the survey. If this Jiig Cal was an early attempt at psychometric testing for careers, it needed a rejiig.

I was the only one in my family who didn't want to qualify into the medical profession, but as a consequence of growing up around doctors, who rightly generate much admiration, I had become a job snob. Deep down I knew I wanted to work in a profession that people admired. My grandfather wanted the same for me, and I could see the pride in his eyes when he told people that his granddaughter was going to study law. I had previously been the black sheep for eschewing medicine, but I was now fighting my way back with my new vocation.

However, after about three weeks of first year at uni, I realised I would be a crappy lawyer, on account of finding law prosaically dull and realising I was out of my depth. When my grandfather started asking me about the tax deductibility of items bought for his retirement wind-turbine business, I was forced to point out to him that we had so far only been learning about family law, and I was only slightly familiar with the Human Fertilisation and Embryology Act 1990. I could offer him an opinion on who the legal father of his child would be if he were opting to be a surrogate mother in Scotland, but tax intricacies were beyond me.

I needed a job that wasn't law. Three-quarters of the way down the Jiig Cal list – far below fish farm manager – a job title caught my eye. Recruitment consultant. Sounded pretty flash. Hey, it had taken my father 20 years as a surgeon to gain the title of consultant, but if I played my cards right, I could have the title by the age of 21. Ha.

That was 2001. I had clear plans to stay in recruitment for a couple of years before getting a *proper* job (and this was even before discovering that recruitment consultants were universally unloved), but things worked out somewhat differently. I was fortunate to get my first job with a business that treated recruitment as the craft that it is, so my training was great. After a couple of years, I was starting to become quite accomplished. I had some great customers, was earning well, and was suddenly tempted to persist in this career. Besides, I couldn't think of anything better to do, and my friends weren't exactly endorsing their jobs either. I worked my way up through the ranks of a couple of firms in London, managing teams of around 15 recruiters.

Aside from the industry reputation, there was a lot I enjoyed about recruitment: the camaraderie, the excitement, the complexity of different tasks, and the opportunity to investigate people and businesses in the pursuit of discovering who fits where.

In 2008 I founded Granite Search and Selection. The business grew to about 60 staff by 2014 and was extremely profitable for our sector.

I gleaned particular enjoyment from the success and growth of the team, seeing them master their profession, puffing out their chests as their confidence grew, and hearing about the life plans they could now make thanks to their achievements. I'm proud that many of our employees have now gone on to set up their own businesses or take up senior positions within other firms.

While I'm still pleased with what we achieved during those years, growing and managing a recruitment business of 60 people exemplified how wonderful and yet horrific employment can be – for the employees and leaders in equal measure. Looking back, I realise how much we could have done differently. All of us.

A lack of self-awareness, and a lack of learning and growth, were the key things that led to creating *unhappy* employment for some of us during that time. Many of the challenges we faced in growing a business, trying to grow as leaders, and managing the engagement of employees, are some of the things that have motivated me to write this book and to try to help others see what I didn't.

I sold my business in 2018 and took some time out, finding myself knee-deep in curious questions from my young children such as *Mummy, why do badgers have heads?* and *How fast does the slowest car on Earth travel?* In between these insightful conversations, I have mentored other business leaders and recruiters, and I've continued my advocacy for supporting women in business and industry. But my primary pursuit has been to delve into the subject of employment happiness, which had quickly become an increasingly enigmatic interest. This purpose and passion led me not only to write this book but also to cofound The Condor Collective, which practises what this book teaches.

On a personal note: I am happily married, live in Surrey and have two children. I play hockey competitively, and I'm keen on health and fitness as well as beer and wine. I love speaking to anyone new, as my years of interviewing people have made me fascinated by different people's lives and beliefs. I have spent the last five years reading and learning, more than ever before, and I'm itching to help more businesses create happier employment.

CHAPTER 1

WHY CHANGE IS ESSENTIAL

WE NO LONGER SELL HEROIN OVER THE COUNTER

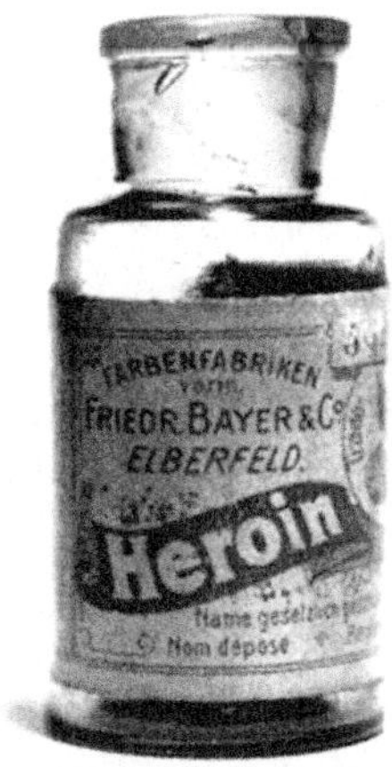

Until 1910, heroin was marketed as a non-addictive cough suppressant. Into the 20th century, smoking was recommended as a treatment for various ailments, including bad breath, throat disease and asthma. And Vin Mariani was a tonic wine, mixed with cocaine, prescribed to maintain a healthy nervous system.

Considering the progress we have witnessed in our lifetime – in everything from medical treatment through to technology, energy, communication, society and behavioural science – it is pretty astonishing that organisational ideology and management have for most businesses remained pretty much unaltered over the last hundred years.

The first era of organisational management structure, as we know it, came at around the turn of the 20th century. Scaled-up mass production processes in factories required managers to assist business owners in organising, directing and controlling their newly expanded workforce. Managers had to find innovative ways of motivating their employees to perform, and they opted for bureaucratic hierarchies with standardised rules. Command and control became the accepted management style.

In 1970 Milton Friedman, Nobel Prize winner for economic sciences, asserted that businesses had no responsibility to the public or to society. Their only social responsibility was to make profit for their shareholders, he maintained. The Friedman Doctrine became the modern interpretation of capitalism. Friedman castigated those organisations that took seriously their 'responsibilities for providing employment, eliminating discrimination, avoiding pollution and whatever else may be the catchwords of the contemporary crop of reformers'.

This was probably music to some businessmen's ears, and many clung on to it. It liberated leaders from difficult moral decisions – from caring – and made them invincible as long as they made profits. This type of command-and-control management, focusing solely on the delivery of profit, overlooked the fact that employees increasingly sought autonomy, meaning and purpose in their work.

Management theory evolved in the mid-1900s, as many employees became knowledge workers rather than manual labourers. Business owners then began to recognise that a pay cheque was not enough – to retain this new type of worker, new forms of motivation and engagement were needed. But even now we are still somewhat unschooled as to what actually motivates us and others.

Thankfully, no one can buy heroin over the counter now, smoking is no longer recommended, and we can't buy wine laced with cocaine. Why, then, are we using management practices and ideology that were best practice 100 years ago?

There are attempts at offering freedom, autonomy and innovation but often only if they are carefully controlled and don't present too much discomfort for businesses. Organisations clearly need more convincing that employee happiness is fundamental in maximising profit and productivity. It's time to question much of what we believe about organisational management and behaviour. It's time to understand how to evolve.

LET'S GET SOCIAL

> 'The secret of change is to focus all your energy not on fighting the old, but on building the new.'
> – Socrates

In building a new world of work, we can approach a transformation of organisations as unencumbered visionaries of the 21st century, thinking and behaving as if we are designing employment completely afresh. We could then fully open our minds to the endless possibilities of achieving happier employment, ignoring the traditionalists, pessimists and opposers who hold Milton Friedman's principles as sacrosanct.

Belief is essential to start the transformation of employment.

What we believe affects what we say and how we behave. If we believe that employment *can* and *should* be happier, that opens up the possibility of change. Only in questioning our beliefs and the way things are do we start to understand that there are different ways for organisations and employees to feel successful, and different ways to generate success.

It's compelling to imagine that, in 20 years' time, more people could be engaged in their jobs than disengaged. Deloitte Global's societal impact survey of 2019, 'The rise of the socially responsible business', showed that nearly all business leaders believe that companies are not only employers but also stewards of society. Furthermore, 95% of leaders stated they were planning to devote significant resources to socially responsible initiatives. Organisations seem to care, and I don't think this is purely lip service. The popularity of caring is gathering momentum, and there are many social initiatives to which organisations can now devote their efforts. However, actually prioritising caring and happiness over other organisational priorities is the reality with which many leaders understandably struggle.

A leader in one of The Condor Collective's workshops commented that he had loved taking the time to reflect, and that he was pumped with ideas on how his organisation could improve its employee engagement. We were revelling in his new-found enlightenment, until he said, 'But now I need to get on with some *actual* work!' We all knew what he meant – we have lived for decades with the reality that tasks with tangible returns are most highly valued. Happiness and engagement are tangible, but they're fighting for priority against our entrenched beliefs and practices.

An increasing number of start-ups are launched with a social purpose in mind. They endeavour to make profits but in ethical ways that contribute to society. The Body Shop is an early example of a social enterprise. Dame Anita Roddick started the business in 1976, and The Body Shop has for over 40 years led campaigns that have changed the laws on animal testing, domestic violence and human trafficking. An enterprise called Invisible Cities trains homeless people to be walking tour guides of their own UK cities. Cafédirect is a Fairtrade coffee company, which invests half its profits back into smallholder farming communities. And Company Shop is a social supermarket offering surplus food at heavily discounted prices to disadvantaged communities.

The growing number of social enterprises is fuelled by increasing pressure, from governments and from society, for businesses to behave more responsibly. Customer demand is possibly the strongest factor – individuals feel more moral responsibility to the environment and to society than ever before, and they are attracted to businesses that demonstrate similar ethics.

Businesses that exist purely for their own gain are becoming ever more unfashionable.

Milton Friedman must be turning in his grave.

There are many consumer models. For example, Tony's Chocolonely tackles modern slavery in Ghana and the Ivory Coast; and TOMS helps communities meet their needs, originally matching every pair of shoes they sold with a donation of shoes to someone in need. These organisations are intent on contributing to society, but their product has to be good too. This is not about being all sizzle and no (vegan) steak. It's about believing that caring for people and the community is a more powerful motivator than ever before.

Another example is UK stalwart Unilever, which has for a long time been seen globally as one of the most sought-after employers. Employees cite the company's ethical and sustainability policies as their primary reason for wanting to join the company. Customers agree – in 2019 Unilever announced that its socially and environmentally led brands were growing 69% faster than the rest of the business and delivering 75% of the company's growth.

Business leaders' mindsets are evidently starting to adapt. Interestingly, though, the focus on helping society is most often external rather than on the internal society of a company, i.e., their employees. There are many merited external causes we can support, but it feels insincere to pledge support for other communities without having our own house in order.

It's great that mindsets are adapting, but it's the action that's important, and this has to be more than social-responsibility window dressing. Action must be motivated by an intrinsic desire to do something better and by the belief that an organisation can do so, while still enjoying profitable returns.

SO WHAT'S HOLDING THIS UP?

If society and consumers are increasingly interested in social value, what's holding leaders back?

DISRUPTING EMPLOYMENT

> 'Minds are like parachutes; they work best when open.'
> – Thomas Dewar, Scottish businessman

Newton's Law of Inertia states that an object at rest or in motion will stay at rest or in motion unless the object is acted upon by an unbalanced force. This is my view of employment. We are trundling along the same course we've been on for decades, hanging in a state of semi-inertia because there hasn't been a strong enough force to punt us onto a new course.

It could be argued that workplace inertia is borne out of our status quo bias and of our natural habit of complaining but doing little to activate change. In the workplace especially, due to the hierarchical command and control we know so well, there's a real reluctance to step out of line and challenge the way things are.

Organisations have advanced, but focus has been technology-orientated: digital systems, artificial intelligence, robotics … almost everything *around* people but not *within* people. It's tempting to hope that the latest software will help, but we need to recognise that there's no quick fix that will eradicate unhappiness at work.

There's a general acceptance in our society that no one likes change.

Will change mean more work?
Will it mean learning new things?
Will I know what I'm doing?
I'm being pushed out of my comfort zone and I might look and feel stupid!

When it comes to making changes to increase happiness, we must accept that the whole purpose of the change outweighs any discomfort and uncertainty we might feel along the way. It will ask us to learn more about ourselves, to see and challenge our behaviour, and to face up to new truths. But it will be worth it.

Creating happier employment is something each of us must work on. It is not only about employers changing, despite what employees may think. It's also not only about employees changing, despite what employers may think. This is about both groups realising that they have blind spots, thoughts, needs, behaviours and motivations, and that they need to change together. We all need to help each other in this. Some may resist change or take longer to grasp it, but it's getting there in the end that is important. Happiness improves wellbeing, mental health, productivity and company profits. From everyone's perspective, it's a change we need.

EXTERNAL INFLUENCE

If we consider the UK's leadership role models, we find 650 of them in the House of Commons, name-calling, jeering and heckling one another in what can only be described as a powerplay playground. That culture would be unfathomable in a modern office. Addressing one another as the *honourable lady* or the *honourable gentleman* doesn't mitigate the condemnation or verbal attack that often follows, yet it is still deemed acceptable in the UK Parliament. This book challenges the outmoded and unconscious practice of behaving in a certain way simply because, *That's the way it's always been.*

> **Elements of good leadership don't eliminate the bad. The bad just has to go.**

The culture in business (and politics) has rightly been put under the spotlight. According to Robert Walters research from 2019, 73% of employees stated that they have left a job due to company culture. Businesses have had to take a fresh look at the *way things work* around here, as a lot of employees don't like that way very much.

Business leaders mustn't be afraid of rejecting outdated business practices, even if they are perfectly used to them. And they must reject processes that are in place simply because leaders secretly enjoy the status, power or importance afforded by them.

This book may be read by leaders and employees of all sizes of businesses, but I'd like to highlight a particularly relevant potential issue for small to medium-sized businesses in creating a happier workplace. Larger businesses have non-executive directors, shareholders, large leadership teams and HR departments, all of which contribute to diversifying beliefs and behaviour as well as holding leaders accountable. SME leaders, on the other hand, often lack those sources of external input, due to constraints around time and cost, or to leaders' very desire to be unaccountable.

As one honest business leader once told me, *You become your own boss so that you don't have to be accountable to anyone.* This can result in business leaders having glaring blind spots when it comes to their own behaviour and business culture, which can prevent them from becoming more accomplished leaders. If we don't look outside or invite other people in, we won't notice the small behavioural indiscretions or the cumbersome processes that compound to systematically erode our culture. Business leaders often don't realise that their culture or leadership is poor until a stream of employees start leaving the company.

If business culture is to evolve, leaders must evolve. Many leaders and managers carry out performance reviews with their team members, often including objectives for growth over a 6- to 12-month period. How many leaders have personal objectives for growth? Why is the number so low? Most leaders set objectives and strategy for the *business*, but it's not the same thing. All leaders must recognise that their personal growth impacts their ability to create happier workplaces.

Leaders can:

- Meet other industry leaders
- Listen to inspirational people
- Attend seminars
- Subscribe to social media forums for articles and blogs
- Read about subjects that interest them
- Learn something new about leadership
- Ask an external consultant to observe your leadership
- Conduct an assessment or survey with your employees

None of this has to take up a huge amount of time, and any time you invest will be worthwhile.

I can vividly remember being so immersed in the day-to-day operational running of my own businesses that it felt suffocating to consider fitting more into the day, least of all non-essential things like seminars and podcasts. I couldn't envisage how those things would have an immediate impact on my business in the way that executing more tasks would. But they do – just in ways we can't measure as easily as our number of sales calls or the decisions made in a meeting. Those of us who have attended amazing presentations or workshops, or have read a book that has changed our beliefs, may remember feelings of enlightenment, clarity and motivation. Leaders need that inspiration more than another hour of operational duties. If we can do it often, the inspiration lasts, and it's exponentially valuable to us and our teams.

It's essential that we carve out time to open our minds. Our employees' happiness – and therefore our productivity and profit – depend on it.

BREAKING FREE FROM AUTHORITARIAN LEADERSHIP

As psychotherapist and writer Claude Steiner once asserted, obedience can often be mistaken for cooperation. Horror stories about management techniques are not uncommon in the recruitment industry. We heard of managers duct-taping phones to the hands of employees to emphasise the importance of spending time making phone calls, or telling innocent trainees they would go to jail if they sent out incorrect CV information. Recruitment was witnessing homogenous, macho, aggressive, authoritarian leadership, which had been revered or at least accepted in all sectors for at least 100 years. So ingrained was the stereotype of the brash, confident leader that some people viewed them as untouchable and infallible business gods.

There was even a blind acceptance that, while we may not have enjoyed having phones duct-taped to our hands, it was probably good for us – a sort of corporate Stockholm syndrome. Many employees have somehow come to accept that a leader might be civil at times and unpleasant at others, but that this is permissible due to the leader's brilliance and the stress of their job.

Authoritarian leadership has led to employees succumbing to a debilitating existence at work. Adults who raise children, vote, fight in wars and are granted mortgages come into the office to find themselves in a pseudo teacher–child relationship, where they might be required to ask to use the bathroom or be chastised in front of their colleagues.

Employees crave an adult culture, where their voice is relevant and they are respected. There is a fundamental difference between being stewarded and being bossed.

There are two sides to this. Employees also must embrace adult autonomy by being accountable for their performance and behaviour. Their failure to do so contributes to leaders' stress, pressure, anxiety or frustration and, ultimately, also their behaviour. We must break this tit-for-tat cycle of poor behaviour generating other poor behaviour and learn that everyone has to take accountability for their own improvement.

Leadership articles and blogs are awash with evidence supporting modern leadership traits that create great culture, including empathy, listening, flexibility, authenticity and building diverse teams. Learned experts also continually develop new leadership styles, searching for the formula that will create amazing success for leaders and organisations.

Faced with the rising pressure of adapting to a more adult style of employment, some leaders will, as a means of counterargument, offer examples of successful autocratic leaders – Jack Welch, Steve Jobs and Donald Trump, to name a few. These leaders were indeed successful, but we should consider whether it was their autocratic leadership that led to success, whether they were successful in spite of it, whether the irascible behaviours only made for better headlines, or whether they simply surrounded themselves with other competent people.

You may have seen the Danny Boyle film *Steve Jobs*, in which we see many displays of Jobs' irascible, selfish and abrasive behaviour. Late in the film, after yet another altercation with his business partner, Steve Wozniak says to Jobs, 'It's not binary – you can be decent and gifted at the same time.' Genius and decency aren't mutually exclusive. And I fear for the happiness of people, and of those around them, who regard decency as a casualty of great leadership.

There is, alas, no formula or specific set of traits that make a leader great. Rather, greatness comes from the ability to adapt our leadership style to the situation and people. However, there are no recently published articles that espouse the merits of autocratic, egotistical, ignorant, arrogant narcissists, so I think we can assume that this style of leadership is on its way out.

We might still take some time to devolve ourselves of such leaders, but it's happening. We are devolving ourselves of authoritarian leadership, and it can't come soon enough.

THE ULTIMATUM

Economist John Galbraith once stated that, when deciding whether to change direction, most people focus on proving there is no need to do so. This epitomises some of the behaviour we see from organisational leaders and employees. Pre-existing strategies, the pressure to meet targets, the fear of things deteriorating, the looming investment of shareholders ... the reasons for sticking with the status quo are numerous. But the longer we leave it, the more gangrenous employment will become.

After decades of command and control, some leaders still find it challenging to envisage any new paradigm of employment, let alone a drive for employee happiness. Some leaders will lament that 20 years ago you *just had to get things done*. You still do, but now there's different and improved thinking on how to ensure things get done. This doesn't mean throwing all previous thinking out of the window. It means being conscious of the elements that are actually serving the modern workforce and those that aren't.

Perhaps changes to employment are slowed because leaders like commanding and controlling. Perhaps employees feel they can't start the organisational equivalent of a coup d'état for fear of receiving a poor reference once they've been fired. Perhaps few leaders back themselves to lead the change successfully, hindered by the fear that failure would be corporate suicide. Perhaps employees haven't yet realised that they are part of the problem.

There's a saying by Neil Ravikant, in the book *Tools of Titans*, that our choice in any situation is to change it, accept it, or leave it. Well, we can't completely abandon employment – at least not until we retire. And we have for too long been accepting things the way they are. We therefore have to change the current situation.

Our consciousness to become better humans is an evolving process. We now look on other historic social injustices with bewilderment, and I hope, some years from now, we will reflect on employment and wonder why we put up with the crappy bits for so long.

WE CAN DO THIS

We've belaboured the critique of past workplace culture long enough. It's time to focus forward.

UNDERSTANDING HAPPINESS

> 'Life is really simple, but we insist on making it complicated.'
> – Confucius

Happiness is a state – a feeling – an underlying sense of contentment. We think our happiness changes depending on a multitude of factors: elements of our demographic, our mood on a particular day, or whether we've had a frustrating interaction on the way to work (damn those people who don't have their tickets ready at the Tube station turnstile).

What affects our general state of happiness can be difficult to define, mostly because we fundamentally misunderstand what makes us happy. When asked about our happiness, we might talk about getting a good job, being promoted, buying a forever home, having a family or buying a nice car. However, 2012 research by Levine and colleagues demonstrates that these achievements have a negligible effect on our baseline state of happiness. We experience temporary peaks of joy, but our overall happiness is not increased. Also, while things like difficult interactions with people cause frustration or resentment, they do not fundamentally lower our baseline of happiness.

Dan Gilbert, Professor of Psychology at Harvard and author of *Stumbling on Happiness*, found the same results. He explains that humans are terrible forecasters of our emotional reactions to things that will happen in the future. We often incorrectly predict what will make us happy or sad. In the workplace we incorrectly forecast that a 30% pay rise would make us happier than a shorter commute, or that a promotion would make us happier than increased annual leave. Our forecasts around our emotions at work are least accurate when they are about money.

The physiological reason behind this is that our brains are new to the need to forecast future happiness. As cavepeople we didn't have to give this much thought, as we were preoccupied with finding our next meal and avoiding death. Our brains haven't yet evolved to make full sense of modern-day life.

> **We should therefore approach our beliefs about our future happiness with a healthy suspicion.**

What we do know is that, to a point, money can buy you happiness. A 2010 study by Nobel prize-winning psychologist Daniel Kahneman and renowned economist Angus Deaton PhD found that a household income of $75,000 would buy you happiness. However, intriguingly, they maintained that income higher than $75,000 didn't *further* increase happiness. The premise was that this amount of money was enough to live on as well as allowing enough to spend on socially rich experiences.

The reason life events don't have as profound an impact on our baseline happiness is an observed tendency in humans called *hedonic adaptation*. Quite simply, this term means that humans *get used to stuff*. We strive for things, and once we have them, they become mundane or everyday, and we settle back to the same baseline of happiness we had before.

Think of a new car you have had. To begin with, you cleaned it, relished the new smell, appreciated the internal parking cameras and felt more special driving around in the car. Three months later, it has remnants of snacks kicking about the footwell, there's algae growing on the rear windscreen and – quite literally – it has lost its shine.

We develop hedonic adaptation to new employers, new jobs, pay rises and more. The honeymoon period is over. Spare a thought for leaders who constantly introduce initiatives to satiate employees' needs. However, the new measures quickly become mundane and therefore turn into employee expectations.

From Chapter 2, we'll look more closely at how we can disrupt hedonic adaptation. For now: we are starting to learn that 'stuff' doesn't genuinely make us happy. So what does?

Leaders and employees can benefit from understanding the results from one of the longest-running studies ever completed to give the most significant and overriding insight. The 'Harvard Study of Adult Development' tracked the lives of 724 men for around 80 years. Researchers contacted the group every two years and asked them questions about their physical and mental health, professional and personal lives, friendships and marriages. Robert J Waldinger, the study's fourth director, popularised the study's research in his TED Talk 'What makes a good life: Lessons from the longest study on happiness'. He reported that good relationships unequivocally keep us happier and healthier, particularly those relationships where we have the ability to count on each other when the going gets tough.

Here's the most important point: this type of relationship isn't exclusive to people we know outside of work.

Relationships in the workplace often become fractured due to misunderstanding, misinterpretation, assumption and unconscious bias. With increased knowledge and the practice of communicating with emotional intelligence, we can restore and build our workplace relationships, leading to a stronger baseline of happiness in employment.

Understanding that our happiness and health depend on these relationships may prompt us to be more conscious of our behaviour, to be a little more receptive of one another, and to deliberately make a little (or a lot) more effort. We discover in later chapters how we can learn to work more effectively with our colleagues – even those we don't truly like – and how our success and potential are reliant on us doing that.

I described happiness in the introduction as a personal El Dorado. The intangible nature of happiness can give it a mythical reputation, but we mustn't get too hung up on looking for it, as doing so can be counterproductive. As Eleanor Roosevelt said: 'Happiness is not a goal, it is a by-product.' It is clear we must focus our efforts on practising the components that contribute most to our happiness and seek to experience them more frequently. We tend to be passive in our approach to happiness, enjoying the feeling of pleasure but rarely consciously noting where specific activities, tasks or people contribute to our happiness.

To understand your own happiness, or that of your team, you can start by establishing your baseline starting point. You can take one of many tests online or simply note how happy you are with your life on a scale of 1 to10. After learning and practising some of the strategies in this book, when you come to retake the test, things will have improved for you and your team. In a world short of happiness metrics in the workplace, here is an easy place to start!

THE HAPPY ROUTE TO SUCCESS

In our lives we often create a *conditional* interpretation of happiness – a common thought that once we've reached a certain point of success, *then* we will be happy.

> **Society has taught us that happiness is a state that is a consequence of success.**

In his book *The Happiness Advantage*, Shawn Achor argues that it's the other way round.

Happiness is actually the precursor for success. This is all backed up by the science of *positive priming*, where researchers found that people perform better when they are primed to feel happier. Priming doesn't involve reminding people of impending targets, behaving rudely and distantly because we're wrapped up in our own self-importance, or saying mean things to people in the ladies bathroom because we're stressed (these are all mine). Positive priming is doing things that get us into a great mindset – a happy mindset. This could be listening to our favourite tunes, eating a favourite lunch, watching cool TikTok videos, looking at photos of our kids or smelling the fresh air outside.

Happiness releases dopamine and serotonin, two of our body's chemicals that regulate mood. Dopamine plays an important role in executive brain function, motor control and motivation. Essentially, when we feel happy, our brains function better and our energy for tasks increases. Several studies have shown that doctors in a positive mood diagnose their patients more accurately and more quickly, and they spend more time with them and write fewer prescriptions. Next time you are going into your doctor, be sure to compliment them on arrival.

You can try positive priming at work. Try it for a week, say, by giving positive feedback to team members, buying your team doughnuts, suggesting everyone leaves early one day for having worked so hard, or getting everyone a round of coffees from a cool café. Any or all of these touches will get everyone feeling better and working more productively.

Stop for a minute and think about a particularly happy day at work. You surely felt more resilient, and you were probably more focused and felt more receptive to others. Maybe you even felt a little invincible? I bet you were more productive that day.

Extensive research has shown that businesses that prioritise employee happiness benefit from increased productivity. Happiness is no longer only a societal nicety – it's an economic necessity.

Despite the evidence, most businesses and employees struggle to depart from the refuted belief:

Productivity leads to success, which generates happiness

The order is in fact quite different:

Happiness improves productivity, which generates success

Traditionally, organisational efforts to increase productivity advocate incentivisation, technology, more systems, setting increased targets, ironing out inefficiencies, and the like. None of this is misdirected, but it's putting the cart before the horse. Can you envision a person who's uninspired, slumped over their desk after an unsavoury altercation with their manager? Now ask them to improve their productivity by working more efficiently. Or incentivise them with a bonus for great productivity. How far does that get anyone towards success? And how happy is that person?

According to Shawn Achor, happy salespeople produce 37% greater sales, and engaged teams generate 21% more profit than disengaged ones. People being happy in their jobs makes businesses and the economy thrive. It's a modern-day solution for productivity.

> **Happiness is by no means the only thing employees need, but it is vital to recognise that the real route to success is in prioritising happiness, not grinding out productivity.**

For anyone who needed convincing that this fluffy, ethereal thinking is the way forward, the proof is in the profits.

CREATING CHANGE

> 'A wise man changes his mind. A fool never will.'
> – Spanish proverb

Scholars debate over whether we can successfully instigate change by changing people's beliefs and then their behaviour, or whether we need to change behaviour first in order to change beliefs. It's perhaps a modern-day business equivalent of *What came first, the chicken or the egg?* Awareness of both our own beliefs and the impact of our behaviour is vital to making change possible.

Let's draw a parallel with a change we've all experienced outside of work. Household recycling has taken place since Roman times, when bronze coins were recycled. It started to gather momentum in the 1900s, when companies such as AG Barr, which manufactures Irn Bru, started paying people for returning their glass drinks bottles. In 2017 Varotto and Spagnolli undertook a study, 'Psychological strategies to promote household recycling'. They found that, of the 70 interventions they examined, the most effective techniques were *social modelling and environmental alterations.*

Social modelling is about how most human behaviour is learned through watching others. We see other people recycling and are inspired to do so ourselves. Environmental alterations are straightforward – we see and understand the damage to the environment if all of our rubbish is sent to landfill.

These two tactics, along with new processes that make recycling easier and cheaper, have meant that the vast majority of people now consciously recycle. Most people used to be pretty apathetic about recycling; now even the thought of disposing of a glass bottle in a normal bin fills most of us with horror.

Similar changes are already starting in employment. We are observing increasing attention to empathetic leadership and employee wellbeing. This spurs more of us to do the same (social modelling), and we are developing an increased understanding of the damage that is being done if we don't make changes (environmental impact). Moreover, we have a better understanding of the financial benefits of happier employment, not only to employees and employers, but also to the economy as a whole.

Legislation is also playing its part. The Companies Act 2006 and the Corporate Governance Code, for example, put the onus on directors to explain how they take the interests of their workforce into account in decision making and to create a culture that aligns company values with long-term strategy.

The recycling example illustrates how beliefs can be transformed, albeit sometimes over decades. At some point in the future, the employee experience of today will be reflected on with the same bewilderment that we now regard a single household bin. The speed at which we get there is up to all of us.

IF A COUNTRY CAN CHANGE ...

In 1972 The King of Bhutan, Jigme Singye Wangchuck, coined the statement 'Gross national happiness is more important than gross domestic product'. He was expressing a philosophy that challenged the conventional materialistic measurement of GDP and sought to create conditions for the development of the most important wealth of all: human happiness. Within 20 years, Bhutan overhauled its infrastructure, doubled life expectancy within its kingdom and enrolled almost 100% of its children in primary school.

In 2019, under the stewardship of Jacinda Ardern, New Zealand released the first ever wellbeing budget, outlining their commitment to:

1. Support mental wellbeing for all New Zealanders, with a special focus on under-24-year-olds
2. Reduce child poverty and improve child wellbeing, including addressing family violence
3. Lift Māori and Pacific incomes, skills and opportunities
4. Support a thriving nation in the digital age through innovation, social and economic opportunities
5. Create opportunities for productive businesses, regions, iwi and others to transition to a sustainable and low-emissions economy

According to Ardern, her government has laid the foundation for not just one wellbeing budget, but for an altogether different approach to government decision making.

If a country as small and economically challenged as Bhutan can challenge the world's entrenched measurement of GDP as the indicator of prosperity, and other highly developed nations are now taking up the baton, this offers great hope for the potential of changing organisations' prioritisation of happiness. A nation's happiness is closely linked to people's satisfaction in their careers. Creating a happy nation is therefore rather dependent on creating happier employment.

If leaders and employees can fathom and adopt the notion that employment can and should be happier, and that every person can contribute positively or negatively to a colleague or customer's happiness, we will start to build a better social justice in the workplace.

TIMING IS EVERYTHING

Biz Stone, the co-founder of Twitter, famously claimed that timing and perseverance, together with many years of effort, can make anyone seem like they've achieved overnight success. Idealab founder Bill Gross, meanwhile, argues that timing is the crucial factor in the success or failure of new businesses. Through analysis and comparison of start-up successes and start-up failures, Gross concluded that timing was the determining factor for success in 42% of cases. This was over and above factors such as the team involved, the idea itself, the business model and the funding achieved.

Gross offers Airbnb as a great example. It's hard to believe now that Airbnb initially experienced two failed launches. They had a good business model and team, but potential investors were convinced that homeowners wouldn't want to rent out their homes to strangers, or that anyone would choose a stranger's apartment over a hotel. But when Airbnb launched for the third time, in 2008, the economic downturn meant that potential guests had less disposable income to spend on hotels, and homeowners needed new ways to make money. At the time of writing, the company is worth $87.55 billion.

> **This isn't only about start-ups – timing is vital to the success of any new strategy.**

There is no doubt that the timing is now perfect for disrupting employment as we know it. We've emerged from a worldwide pandemic, and employees are not only questioning *how* they are working but also *why*, which has forced businesses to accelerate their flexibility and attentiveness to the employee experience.

Even before the pandemic, ESG (environmental, social, governance) standards were of increasing importance to businesses. Governments are inviting change with amendments to the Corporate Governance Code and Section 172 of the Companies Act, which place greater onus on publicly owned businesses to consider all stakeholders – rather than only shareholders – in their decision making. The work has come together on the Sustainable Development Goals and the Paris Agreement, but change is slow. Change needs the momentum of businesses that employ the world's elite talent in great numbers to help drive this change, and to benefit from doing so.

At the time of writing, Gallup estimates that the cost of poor management and lost productivity from disengaged employees approaches $8.8 trillion worldwide – the equivalent of 9% of the world's GDP. Leaders probably don't notice the trillions being lost. That's because traditional management practices don't usually cause overt damage. Some of the practices only make employees a little less engaged, a little less loyal and a little less productive. But a little less of all those factors ultimately adds up to a lot less profit.

The science of psychology offers lots of new insights for the workplace, and we need these insights now more than ever. There's dissatisfaction with current hiring, there's a worldwide skills shortage, and the majority of employees are not actively engaged with their workplaces. And, as discussed in the previous section, we are at last enjoying a time when many leaders are ready to change their mindsets.

As the former Chief Executive of GE, Jack Welch, said: the end is in sight when change occurs more slowly inside an organisation than on the outside.

Win some, lose some

I started my first business in October 2008 – the month after Lehman Brothers declared bankruptcy. Their demise was one of the defining moments of the 2008 financial crisis, and shortly after we saw videos of people carrying their belongings out of Lehman's buildings, I was sitting in an office with my then boss, resigning from my job. He, understandably (if manipulatively), chose to emphasise that this might not be the best time to start my own business. As it turned out, it was absolutely the best time. My personal circumstances helped – I had saved some money so could afford to be without an income for a while (something I would urge all would-be entrepreneurs to consider before starting up!). As other recruitment businesses were having to contend with cumbersome overheads, redundancies and huge cash flow concerns, I only had to contend with my own sanity, while working at my kitchen table for eight months before I found a paying customer. This afforded me the time to set up everything I needed. I wasn't torn apart by how much work I was missing out on, because there wasn't any. By the time the market recovered, I was ready to go. And go I did.

Conversely, in 2015, when my business had around 60 in the team, my co-founder and I decided it would be wise to diversify our industry focus. We wanted to ensure we could manage the next recession in construction by counterbalancing it with strength in another industry. We decided to branch into oil and gas. After doing our due diligence, we felt confident we understood the oil and gas recruitment terrain. We hired a guy from Aberdeen, relocated him to London, and waited for him to bring his database into the business. Two weeks later, he absconded from the apartment we had rented for him, taking his signing-on bonus and non-existent database with him. We never heard from him again.

Shortly after this episode, we re-recruited, hiring three excellent people, only for the oil and gas industry to sink into recession and the oil price to absolutely tank. We pivoted and persevered for some time – too long, on reflection – and all in all sank about two years and £400k into a failed attempt.

This was a tough lesson and taught me new levels of appreciation for due diligence, making tough decisions and the importance of timing. Thankfully, the failure of this venture didn't damage the success of our core business, and we continued to help grow careers inside our business and for our clients. And of course, just about any setback can be reframed into a positive learning experience. You win some; you lose some.

CHAPTER SUMMARY

When a new truth enters our existence, it can feel cataclysmic, especially when it's something we have never thought to question before.

Examples:

- Discovering that there are people in this world who wash the dishes fully before putting them in the dishwasher
- Finding out that Santa doesn't exist
- Discovering that a penny dropped from the top of a skyscraper won't injure someone below

Beliefs are shattered in an instant. However, finding out that the truths we held so dear are not actually truths – that they are only what we have been led to believe until now – can be viewed as a positive experience. Moving forward, we have the opportunity to see things in a clearer way and to recognise that the previous truth wasn't serving us as well as it could.

It's not our fault if we haven't fully questioned our leadership or our employment so far. Why would we? We're all in a huge cultural melee of acceptance of the way things are, and we rarely afford ourselves the opportunity to stop and reflect (mostly because we are too busy trying to hit those damned productivity targets).

However, until a group of people disrupts the culture, it won't be disrupted. And employment won't become happier.

KEY REMINDERS FROM THIS CHAPTER

- We no longer believe heroin is medicinal. In the future we will probably be wondering why we didn't question workplace culture sooner. Challenge your beliefs; uphold your values.
- Individuals and businesses are increasingly drawn to organisations with a social purpose. That social purpose can be improving workplace happiness.
- Disrupting employment requires an investment into how we think, feel and behave in the workplace. It won't be fixed with new software. We need to question and adapt our beliefs and behaviour.
- We need to check we are getting enough external influence to challenge our thinking. Whether it's from joining leadership forums, listening to podcasts or networking with others, external influence is a stimulus of ideas and an inspiration for growth.
- Modern leadership is about embracing culture, empathy, vulnerability and listening skills, in addition to many solid management practices of the past. Infallibility, arrogance and narcissism are redundant leadership traits.
- Happiness is an underlying state. Look for experiences and relationships that will enrich your baseline for happiness rather than adopting an over-reliance on peaking moments of joy.
- Be aware of hedonic adaptation. The speed at which we get accustomed to things leads us to continuously look for the next spike of joy. Before long, we are on the treadmill of happiness.
- Happiness equals productivity, which equals success. Explore the things that add to your happiness. Focus on those and stop chasing conditional happiness.

- The time for change is now. If entire countries can change by prioritising happiness, so can businesses.

Before we can start to envisage employees singing kumbaya around a campfire and brushing each other's hair in a euphoric state of cultural and social heaven, we must turn our attention to the behavioural change, tools and techniques we need to get there. The case for happier employment has been made; now we must galvanise our thoughts and inspiration into action.

CHAPTER 2

EMOTIONAL INTELLIGENCE

> 'Knowing others is intelligence; knowing yourself is true wisdom. Mastering others is strength; mastering yourself is true power.'
> – Lao Tzu

Our happiness or unhappiness in our jobs is directly connected to how we feel about our work, our colleagues and our workplace. It is therefore a highly emotional forum. We might feel overlooked, underpaid, disrespected, like we don't belong. We may feel restricted, unchallenged, micromanaged, unclear of expectations. All of these things illustrate needs, thoughts and emotions that affect our engagement and happiness. If we learn to recognise and manage our own needs, thoughts and emotions, as well as learning to understand those of others, we can achieve a far more harmonious way of working together. This is key to a happier workplace. Currently, we are usually not adept at seeing ourselves objectively, recognising when we have unhelpful thoughts or unmet needs in the workplace, or acknowledging when we are displaying toxic behaviour.

Emotional intelligence is a misunderstood term, which leaders might find themselves using when browbeating underperforming employees, all the while failing to see the irony of their own behaviour. In this chapter I will help you see yourselves more objectively.

In his book *Emotional Intelligence*, Daniel Goleman cites the Harvard Business School research that determined that emotional intelligence counts for twice as much as both intelligence and technical skills in determining who will be successful.

Success is positively affected by stronger relationships, comfortable conflict, increased collaboration, psychological safety and resilience - all benefits of strong emotional intelligence.

Getting our heads around the idea of improving *skills* – such as presenting, handling customer calls or writing strategy – is one thing. Getting our heads around improving our *behaviour* and *emotions* can be more challenging. This is partly because the historic belief has been that attitude, emotions and behaviour are natural, unadaptable personality traits. Schools, colleges, universities and employers therefore haven't dedicated much – if any – time to educating the current workforce in emotional intelligence. It's not the educator or organisation's fault; the term emotional intelligence was first conceived in 1990, so we are still warming up to the concept.

Skilfully managing emotions and behaviour is the game changer of happier employment.

I often think that there are few truly terrible people in this world. Yet we sometimes feel that our colleagues or managers have been handpicked to sabotage our daily lives. We don't choose who we work with, and we are in pressured environments with deadlines, standards, expectations and high stakes. This is a boiling pot that can test anyone's emotions and behaviour. People aren't terrible – far from it – but at times they can appear to be due to the challenges in managing their own and other people's emotions.

With dedication, deliberate practice and tuition, we can become extremely accomplished at anything, including *our emotions* and *how we behave*. If you have a propensity to react angrily, if you feel anxious in certain situations, if you say passive-aggressive things from time to time, or if you struggle to shift yourself out of a bad mood … all of these things are not you. They are simply how you let yourself feel and behave.

Open yourself up to the idea that you can take every ingrained thought, behaviour and emotion and adapt it to how you want it to be.

When we talk of emotional intelligence, we are referring to someone's ability to acquire knowledge of and understand emotions. I struggled to understand this at first – if I wanted to improve my behaviour, why wasn't it called *behavioural intelligence*? I rationalised the term by understanding that often our most dislikeable or destructive behaviours are preceded by emotion. Our emotions feel so everyday to emotional-intelligence novices that they are scarcely detectable. Our opportunity to make a good choice of behaviour is therefore completely determined by our ability to notice, understand and manage our emotions.

To give ourselves the best opportunity for success in relationship management – one of the key aspects of creating happiness in our lives – we must first understand a little more about our brains.

THE BRAIN

The amygdala is the part of the brain where emotions precede rational thought. It's our threat sensor – one we have relied on to keep us alive since we were living in caves and fighting large predators with sharp sticks.

Our amygdala instinctually gets to work first, that is, before our prefrontal neocortex – where we regulate actions and emotions – has had a chance to intervene. Problematically, our amygdala can't distinguish between real threats and perceived threats. It therefore treats hurtful feedback in the workplace as a threat to our self-worth and status, and we can react as we would to the onslaught of a sabre-toothed tiger.

Our objective is to control our amygdala as quickly as we can. We don't need to feel threatened when someone challenges us – we can train ourselves out of that type of reaction. Life is a lot happier when we learn to observe and manage what our brain is instinctually making us think, feel and do.

SELF-AWARENESS – KNOWING ONE'S EMOTIONS

Research by organisational psychologist Tasha Eurich has shown that self-awareness is a rare quality: 95% of us think we are self-aware, but only 10–15% of us actually are. We are unaware about our self-awareness – quite the vicious circle.

Simply put, self-awareness is the habit of recognising how we think, feel or behave in specific situations. These situations can be acute – spikes of emotion triggered by something specific; or chronic – longer-lasting undertones of emotion, such as stress or resentment, which simmer under the surface and subtly affect how we feel, think and behave.

Self-awareness is theoretically simple. As with many simple concepts, though, it is actually quite hard to put self-awareness into practice, particularly because we are rather wedded to our patterns of emotions and behaviours – so much so that we don't really notice them.

Developing a high degree of self-awareness allows us to question and control our thoughts or emotions *as we experience them*. If we can develop our ability to do this, we give ourselves the first opportunity to slow down and choose how we want to behave. We start to retrain our brains away from our instinctual reactions, to form new patterns of behaviour.

WHAT'S IN THE WAY OF BETTER SELF-AWARENESS?

We learned in Chapter 1 that we often misunderstand our own happiness. Here we look deeper into other psychological research that illustrates other misunderstandings that can get in the way of developing self-awareness.

HUMANS ARE ILLOGICAL AND IRRATIONAL

This was illustrated in a challenge called the *ultimatum game*. A person is given a sum of money – let's say $20 here – by a stranger and is told that they can keep it, but only if they split it with a friend. The one other condition is that both parties keep the money only if the friend accepts what they are offered. Rationally, everyone is better off if they make a deal.

When the chosen friends are offered $1 of the $20, many reject it. Further studies have shown that the friend had to be offered between 30% and 50% in order to make the deal.

Why would the second person not accept that something is better than nothing?

One consideration is that people automatically fall into a commercial mode when money is concerned. Negotiating and bartering are expected, even if someone walks away with nothing (which happens frequently in business). Would the outcome have been different if they were asked to split a loaf of bread? Perhaps. Another explanation lies in people's perception of fairness. Would the only fair solution be to split the $20 evenly?

What would you do in this situation?

Concepts such as fairness or unfairness are simply thoughts. We subjectively decide what we think is fair or unfair, based on past experiences, the values we were taught throughout our lives, our own personal circumstances or our beliefs. Fairness is an opinion, and it's all too often very emotionally charged because we feel so entrenched in our perspective. Our opinion on what is fair and what is unfair can also change if we have acquired further information and feel the circumstances have changed.

Disney fairness

When Robin Williams agreed to voice the character of the Genie in Disney's 1992 feature film *Aladdin*, he accepted $75,000 instead of a more typical fee of $8 million. Williams was keen to be part of the Disney animated tradition and to leave a legacy for his children. However, once the movie had grossed $504 million at the box office, Williams and his agent reopened the conversation with Disney over his pay, allegedly because it felt unfair in light of the incredible success of the movie. Disney subsequently agreed to increase his pay to $1 million.

Imagine if you negotiated a pay rise and were extremely happy with it. Then later the same week, you discovered that someone of similar experience, tenure and performance level was paid more than you. Having originally thought your deal was great, would you suddenly feel your deal was unfair? Is it fair or unfair for people to be paid at different levels for fulfilling the same job function?

If we can start to reflect on our thoughts and feelings, we give ourselves the opportunity to challenge why we think and feel the way we do. This gives us space to calm our amygdala, consider different perspectives and choose our next move.

OUR OWN PERSPECTIVE

All too often we feel our own perspective or opinion is the only viable one. Perhaps we have left a meeting and spoken to a close friend or colleague about how unreasonable the other party was, or that *they just don't get it*. Our beliefs, thoughts and practices are carved and engrained over our lifetimes, which is why it's so difficult for us to fathom that there's a different truth that others hold equally strongly to be 'right'. Something that seems a huge injustice to us might not matter in the slightest to someone else. Or something that is deeply upsetting for us might be only mildly aggravating for others. If we can start to look a little more objectively at our thoughts and emotions, the opportunity for understanding ourselves and others opens up in front of us.

THE DRAMA TRIANGLE

Stephen Karpman created The Drama Triangle in 1968. Its purpose was to help people understand the personas people adopt when they find themselves in difficult situations. Because of our instinctual emotions and habitual behaviours, we are often unaware of when we fall victim to one of these personas.

The Drama Triangle looks like this:

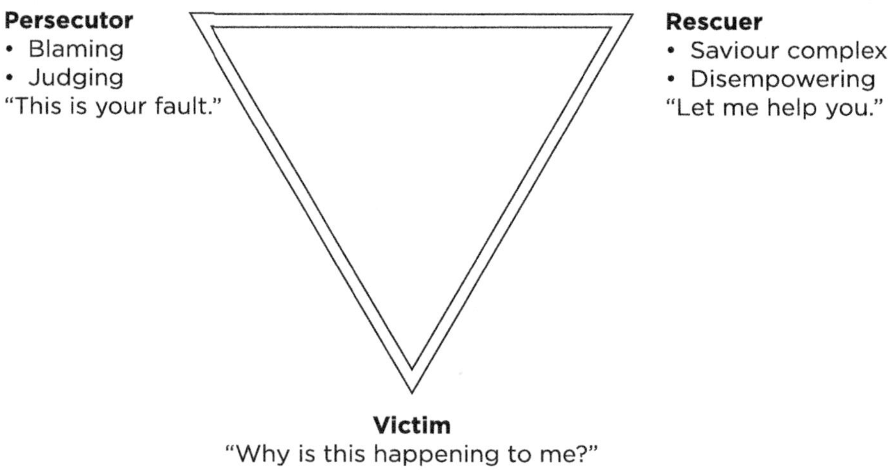

The victim persona is characterised by the phrase *Poor me.* It's when someone has a tendency to think things like:

These things always happen to me.

Why are people being so mean?

Life isn't fair.

If we hide what we need and don't speak up, we become victims by our own hand. If our belligerence causes us to become ostracised, we may believe we are the victim, whereas in fact our behaviour created the outcome.

The rescuer persona is someone who swoops in in hero-like fashion, offering temporary solutions to the victim's problems and often reaping a fantastic self-esteem boost in doing so. Unfortunately, this type of help is often counterproductive. It only temporarily solves the problem and does not allow the victim to help themselves in the future. A well-known analogy for this: a rescuer is someone who will bring fish each day for someone who is hungry, but if they taught the person to fish, they'd be fixing the root cause of the problem.

The persecutor persona is characterised as the frustrated bully – someone who always thinks:

They're wrong, I'm right

You have to do what I say.

It can be someone who feels they are better, smarter or stronger, and who jumps to attack mode when confronted with frustration, inconvenience or pain.

These personas have interesting dynamics: people can find themselves swapping from victim to persecutor to rescuer, all in the course of one conversation.

The original idea of Karpman's model was to:

- Generate understanding of which persona we identify with most naturally
- Raise consciousness about when we are falling into certain personas
- Allow us to recognise the disadvantages of doing so

Observing and catching ourselves in certain behaviours is great, but being able to implement a reframed way of thinking is even better. In 2005 David Emerald Womeldorff created The Empowerment Dynamic, which sees the role of victim develop into *creator*, persecutor into *challenger* and rescuer into *coach*. You'll notice this flips the triangle upside down:

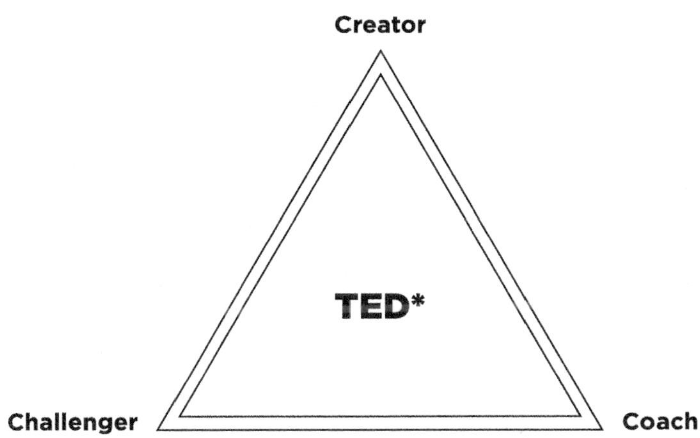

The Empowerment Dynamic

Here's how these transformations work.

From victim to creator

Instead of *Poor me*, think *I believe in myself and can be responsible for the outcome I want.*

Focus on outcomes rather than problems, become a survivor, and focus on what there is to be grateful for and the strengths you have, to get to an outcome you want.

From persecutor to challenger

Instead of intimidating and blaming, think constructive and assertive.

Encourage assertiveness and accountability in others and show them how this can be done constructively.

From rescuer to coach

Instead of *Let me fix this for them*, think *How can I help this person make informed choices?*

Ask: *What do you want to happen?* or *How do you think you can make this outcome better?*

We see the victim competition in many work conversations. Employees trade stories of who works the longest hours, who has the most difficult manager, or who has the toughest job. While some people with the victim persona generally struggle with self-sabotage – perhaps they've suffered a particular trauma, or they lack self-confidence and optimism – others adopt it simply because there is a workplace inclination for sympathy-seeking and shielding from or deflecting blame.

Victim is also the go-to persona when people don't get what they expect or want, or when they feel something is unfair. Victim mentality spreads negativity and can be manipulative, with the victim commanding attention from others.

Instead of falling into victim mentality, take responsibility for shifting out of that status. There will always be setbacks, disappointments or disagreements, but our mentality and approach to a situation are up to us. We'll be creating a happier environment for everyone if we choose to hold ourselves accountable for being a creator rather than victim.

DEFENSIVENESS, JUSTIFICATIONS AND EXCUSES

When we make mistakes, we regularly say, *No one's perfect*, or *We're only human!* We nonchalantly embrace humans as wonderfully imperfect and accept that we all have weaknesses. But when weaknesses are applied to us – in feedback, for example – most of us feel hurt and get busy with defensiveness, excuses or blame – all behaviours that distract us from hearing important information that would benefit our self-awareness. These reactions are fight or flight responses because we feel threatened and our amygdala has got to work.

Even when someone delivers feedback well (a learned skill we tackle in Chapter 8), it's natural for us to feel hurt. We simply don't like hearing feedback that challenges our competence, likeability or status.

What's in the way of developing better self-awareness? Our brains are. Our emotional reactions are. Our patterns of behaviour are. Let's look at how we can improve.

STRATEGIES FOR SELF-AWARENESS

The following techniques for achieving strong self-awareness may feel simplistic, but please don't overlook them. You will be pleasantly surprised by the results.

Notice, name, reason

Notice when you feel an emotional reaction

If you feel joyful, you will probably feel a lightness and excitement.

If you feel threatened, you might notice your heart pounding in your chest, your breath quickening and your palms becoming sweaty.

Name the emotion

Embrace the language of a five-year-old, for example, *I'm happy/sad/angry.*

Go deeper. Do you feel frustrated, shameful, fearful, neglected, apprehensive, rejected, appreciated, valued, enriched, free or trusted?

Here you need to be accurate with what you feel, so you might need to ask yourself several times if you are convinced you have the right label.

> **The simple act of labelling negative emotions helps to diffuse the strength of the emotion.**

Reason: consider what's behind the emotion

Why do I feel this way?

It can be hard to identify the reason behind an emotion, and the reason is often not what you first think it is. It can therefore help to explore your reasoning with someone else who knows you well. Try to avoid blaming others – remember that only you are in charge of your emotions, and someone else in would potentially have a different reaction. The truth about your feelings lies only with you.

Justifying distance

The main critical feedback I received as a leader in my first business was that I was distant. My idea of a work relationship was hearing enough about people's personal lives to know the names of their partners or a bit about their background, and I expected people to be satisfied with the same level of knowledge about me. I also regarded the workplace as a place to carry out focused, disciplined work, free of unnecessary social distractions. In short, I misunderstood the value of strong personal relationships.

As part of our learning and development, one year my leadership team undertook an exercise where we invited feedback from peers, bosses and team members. This was both statistical and anecdotal, and my penchant for keeping people at arm's length was flagged.

My response? I justified away. My inner monologue was working overdrive with thoughts such as:

I can't be good at everything.

I don't need close relationships with people at work.

I don't have time to socialise when I'm at work.

Having closer relationships would make me a less effective leader because I value a degree of separation so I can have difficult conversations when needed.

I struggled most with the belief that adapting my behaviour in one area would have a negative impact on my effectiveness as a leader elsewhere. I see now how I could have significantly improved my leadership and raised my potential as a leader by understanding and investing more in the value of relationships at work. I could also still carry out difficult conversations where necessary – it wasn't one or the other. In fact, the deeper relationships I have now make those conversations far easier and more impactful for the team.

The lesson for me was that I needed to listen to what they needed and to work out how to give it to them, rather than justifying my need for the existing behaviour.

Retrospectively unpicking your behaviour and emotions is a great way to develop your self-awareness.

Try thinking of a situation recently where you have experienced a form of negative emotion and then work through these questions:

- How did you behave / what happened?
- What emotions were you feeling?
- What thoughts were you thinking?
- What did you need that you didn't have? For example, understanding, freedom, appreciation, belonging.

If you work through this exercise each time you experience an emotionally charged situation, you will start to understand more about the thoughts and needs you have and how they affect your emotions and behaviour. Next we need to learn how to control them.

SELF-REGULATION – MANAGING ONE'S EMOTIONS

> 'If someone tried to take control of your body and make you a slave, you would fight for freedom. Yet, how easily you hand over your mind to anyone who insults you. When you dwell on their words and let them dominate your thoughts, you make them your master.'
>
> – Epictetus

Shotts Prison

When I was a law student in Edinburgh in the late 90s, I studied criminal law, and the course included a visit to Shotts Prison. Shotts was Scotland's high-security prison, housing more than 200 murderers. We had a brief conversation with the prison governor before being taken to a lounge room. There was a pool table, Sky TV, a gym and a woodworking area, with a few men milling around. I had expected to be talking to prisoners about the criminal justice system through telephones and bulletproof glass, but that appeared to be only what happened in the movies. In Scotland they simply invite you in for a face-to-face chat with the ten highest-risk offenders in the prison.

I was petrified.

We were introduced to a group and were able to ask them questions about their experience of the court system and sentencing. We were also desperately curious about their crimes and eventually asked what had driven them to murder someone. The conversation I remember most vividly was with a 30-something-year-old man, who proudly displayed three large scars on his face. He said he was part of the Glasgow mafia, and we didn't doubt it. He had been convicted of murdering a man outside a nightclub. The reason: 'I didn't like the way he looked at me. He was disrespecting me.'

It felt so irrational to us that this perceived threat to status had resulted in this man 'losing it' and ruining his life. He, though, spoke as if it had been worth it.

So strong is our evolutionary need for status that we see mild versions of the above in our everyday work lives. We must develop our ability to regulate our emotions and beliefs so that we avoid making a poor behavioural choices.

Self-regulation is the ability to manage disruptive emotions and impulses.

This involves the process of pausing before responding – giving ourselves time to decide on how we want to feel and how we want to behave. We know we are starting to self-regulate when we notice that we are not responding impulsively.

Self-regulation is not only about anger and frustration. Our ability to self-regulate allows us to bounce back from failure, to stay calm under pressure and to motivate ourselves. Biological impulses drive our emotions, but we get to decide what we do with them.

STRATEGIES FOR SELF-REGULATION

Saying it out loud

After identifying the emotion you feel and naming it, say how you feel, out loud, even if you are on your own. This has an amazing effect of instantly helping to de-escalate the emotion you are feeling. If you are with someone else, bringing feelings into the conversation will give the other person the opportunity to adjust their behaviour to help you manage yours.

If you're not in a comfortable environment to say it out loud, say it in your head.

Composing yourself

When we see a professional footballer stepping backwards from the penalty spot, preparing for their run-up to strike the penalty, we often see them pause for a few seconds. At this point, I'm sure there are few footballers in the world who don't feel a surge of emotion – the fear of missing the penalty.

What do we see them do? They compose themselves. They breathe deeply, focus intently on the goal, and dispel from their mind the jibes and jeers of the crowd.

When you next feel a surge of emotion, connect with this image of being a professional footballer about to take a penalty. The process is the same for you.

Buying time to compose yourself

We need time to settle our amygdala and enable our rational brain to re-engage. Ideally, you need about 60 to 90 seconds, but take anything you can get. If you find yourself in a conversation that you find emotionally charging, you can ask to take a break, excuse yourself to go to the bathroom or make a cup of tea.

If you are in the middle of a meeting and there is no real opportunity to break out, do the next best thing: take the time for a couple of deep breaths.

Deep breathing

This slows your heart rate and helps control the physiological response your body generates in times of a heightened emotional state. A popular framework is box breathing, where you can imagine tracing around the side of a box to control your breaths in and out. Breathe in for four counts (going up the side of the box), hold the breath for four (going along the top of the box), breathe out for four (going down the side of the box), and then hold that breath for four counts. This is how Navy SEALs breathe in times of extreme stress, so it should work for us.

In the same way that your amygdala sends messages to your body to get ready for fight or flight, your body sends messages back to your brain. When we deliberately slow our breathing, we are sending the message to our brain that the threat has gone and we can stand down.

Positive self-talk

Positive self-talk is a particularly useful strategy for dealing with fear and anxiety. Before a big presentation, an important client meeting or that all-important penalty, you can say to yourself *You've got this, or Come on!*

The words themselves may feel false or forced at first, but positive self-talk is rewarding and will help you shift your mindset. It's undoubtedly what those footballers are doing before taking their penalties.

Cognitive reframing

In short, cognitive reframing is a fancy way of saying we can take a fresh look at something we're feeling or thinking and challenge the way we interpret it, thereby changing the way we feel about it.

Reframing imposter syndrome

In my current business, before we carried out our first workshop, I was anxious. We believed our content was good, but we had never run a workshop before. We didn't know the group we were doing it with well at all, and one of our client's board members was going to be in the meeting.

My business partner said to me, 'This is the last time we will ever be people who have never delivered a workshop before. Everything will be different after this.'

Her point was that there was something uniquely special about this moment, and her words helped to turn anxiety into vision and excitement.

In any situation, we have the choice to derive a positive or a negative interpretation of other people's words or actions. We are hardwired to look for the threats in situations, which is how we have survived for so long as a species. Our brain is still evolving, and we need to continue to retrain it into a more positive style of thinking.

Let's say you are disappointed not to have been invited to a meeting at work. You probably start to question why, perhaps thinking you are no longer going to be involved in that project or aren't considered good enough to be part of the team. These negative interpretations are common, but we can help to regulate our emotions and behaviours with the simplest of strategies: *assume positive intent* (API). Rather than allowing your brain to jump to the worst interpretations, retrain it to jump to the best. For example:

- Perhaps you haven't been invited to this meeting because you have been earmarked for a different landmark project.
- Perhaps you weren't invited because your manager was conscious that you had too much work with other projects and was looking out for your well-being.
- It could even be that someone noticed this meeting was going to be held on your birthday and wanted to surprise you by giving you the day off.

A variation on API is the adage called Hanlon's razor, which states, *Never attribute to malice that which is adequately explained by stupidity.* Perhaps someone simply forgot to invite you to that meeting.

Cognitive reframing helps regulate our emotions by driving us to consider and try to choose a more positive thought. By embracing a healthy curiosity for the facts and an attitude where we assume positivity, we can avoid unnecessary conclusions that impact our happiness.

EMPATHY - RECOGNISING EMOTIONS IN OTHERS

While the first two elements of emotional intelligence are about our needs, thoughts and emotions, the final two are about those of others.

Empathy is the celebrity name drop of 21st-century leadership – it is frequently ranked as the number-one leadership skill. Data collected by the London School of Economics found that those with empathic leaders reported higher levels of engagement (76%) than those with less empathic leaders (32%).

Empathy is striving to understand someone's feelings and perspective.

Empathy is multifaceted, but I believe that management and leadership articles have overhyped *emotional* empathy, to the point that many of us would question if we were narcissists if we didn't shed tears at least once a week.

Cognitive empathy is less renowned, despite the fact that it is the type we use most frequently. Cognitive empathy is where we understand the thoughts and feelings of another person without necessarily feeling the emotions ourselves. For example, it's when you are watching a movie and you suddenly realise that the good guy also has wicked intentions. You understand what the other person is thinking. You don't need to feel that wickedness with them – you simply understand their thoughts.

Cognitive empathy is particularly useful in certain situations in the workplace. For example, if you are mediating a discussion between two conflicting team members, you will use cognitive empathy to understand both parties' perspectives. You don't want to use only emotional empathy here, as you would find yourself too close to the situation.

Empathic leaders are approachable. They make employees feel valued and safe because they believe the leader has seen things from their perspective. Perspectives are not about right and wrong, or agreeing with someone or not. They are simply how one person see things. Therefore, the more that leaders can equip themselves with a variety of perspectives, the better their communication and decision making will be.

Here's an important point to remember: there's a difference between striving to understand how someone feels in a particular situation and determining how we would feel in the same position. For example, if someone is deeply upset because their dog has died, cognitive empathy is to get into their shoes and understand their grief. It's not to determine how we would feel in the same situation – perhaps we don't love animals. Conversely, emotional empathy is about connecting with someone's emotion, not judging the circumstances of the emotion. We can empathise more effectively by remembering a time when we felt the same anxiety, grief, disappointment or anger, but in different circumstances.

Either type of empathy is not about being a walkover or trying to please everyone. It is also not sympathy, where we feel sorrow or pity for people. Put simply, if we can understand how people think and feel, we can then begin to help them manage and regulate their own thoughts, feelings and actions.

Maths test

A friend of mine at school was a sensitive soul, and she had high expectations of herself. When we both received the results of a maths test, I celebrated at achieving 65%. My friend, meanwhile, burst into tears and I leant over to console her for her poor result. However, when I saw her paper, I was surprised to see she'd scored 68%. My empathy turned to embarrassment – I was proud of 65%, yet she was devasted by a higher mark! I found it difficult to empathise because I would have been delighted with her result. I think I told her as much, which didn't help her regain her composure.

While her emotional self-regulation had fallen off a cliff, I had completely failed to empathise. Looking back, if I had sidelined my own assessment of a successful score, I could have empathised more effectively. If I had tuned in to her disappointment, based on *her* subjective standards and expectations, perhaps by thinking of a time when I had been similarly disappointed, I would have truly been putting myself in her shoes.

STRATEGIES FOR EMPATHY

Unplug and really listen

Give people your undivided attention. Put your phone away, don't interrupt, and sit in the feeling with them. When you empathise with someone, it's not about fixing or trying to make light of a situation. It's about sitting in the emotion with the person for a while and acknowledging their thoughts and feelings. This is where you truly connect with people.

Check for understanding

Once you have listened for a while, you can check you are understanding the person correctly, for example: *It sounds like you are feeling anxious at the moment.* Notice here that you are naming their emotion – the same technique you use in self-awareness for identifying your own emotions. If you have misjudged that emotion, the person can put you right.

Imagine your colleague was a close friend

We have different relationships with our work colleagues, and we like some people more than others. Borrow the kind of empathy you feel for close friends, though, and apply it to your team or colleagues. This will help you tune more fully into their perspective and reduce bias.

Remember that empathy goes both ways

Leaders have difficult choices to make, and it is impossible to meet everyone's needs simultaneously. Employees need to practise empathy for leaders, by considering their emotions, the challenges of their role, and the pressures of their decisions and actions. Ask them how they feel. Few people do, but understanding each other doesn't need to be top down.

RELATIONSHIP MANAGEMENT

While self-regulation is about managing or controlling our own emotions and behaviours, relationship management is about managing the emotions and behaviours of others. It is imperative to tackle our learning and development of each of the domains in turn, starting with self-awareness.

There is little chance of managing relationships well if we have no idea or consideration about what we or others are feeling and we can't prevent ourselves from behaviourally losing it amongst our teams. Successfully managing others' spiralling emotions and behaviours rightly requires us to have a modicum of calm.

> **Highly developed relationship management allows people to coach, influence and inspire others, to encourage good collaboration and manage conflict when it arises.**

STRATEGIES FOR RELATIONSHIP MANAGEMENT

Relationship management has to be the most difficult domain in which to create specific strategies. Success in this domain not only practises the dextrous combination of self-awareness, self-regulation and empathy. It also puts these factors in scenarios that demand expertise in communication, collaboration, vision and purpose, creating goals, managing expectations, coaching, and many other skills.

Rest assured that your skills in managing relationships will improve with continued practice in the three parts of emotional intelligence, which essentially act as feeders to improve relationship management.

1. Showing some emotion

However far down the path we are towards skilful emotional management, talking about our own emotions will instantly strengthen our personal relationships.

I can vividly remember the day my leadership coach shared some personal information about a health diagnosis her father had recently received. She was usually careful not to share much of her personal life, as she didn't want to detract attention from her coachee. After sharing her news with me, though, she asked if that made me feel closer to her.

The answer seemed obvious – of course I did. I cared that she was going through something difficult and was sad about it. Turns out this was her way of illustrating to me that, if I didn't share what was going on with me, I would remain a distant, disconnected leader. As such, I would not only miss out on understanding the emotions of others, as they would be reluctant to share with me, but I would also starve them of the opportunity to truly bond with me.

2. Emotional contagion

Emotions pass between people like a virus. Research has shown that putting an actor in with a group of people and instructing him to engage positively with them not only favourably infected their moods – the tasks they were completing as a group also improved.

Setting the emotional tone for an interaction is a great responsibility, because it means we are stimulating the emotional state of another person. Someone who is dominant in a conversation should pay particular attention to the fact that others are listening, watching and absorbing their mood.

When you have strong awareness and control over your emotions and behaviours, you can have a profoundly positive impact on the culture within your organisation.

3. Adapting with integrity

Another key paradigm of this leadership era is to lead with authenticity. We know that a skill of great managers and leaders is the ability to adapt to the group or situation they find themselves in. And integrity and remaining true to our values is imperative for relationship management.

The term *social chameleon* describes someone who adapts their persona based on who they are talking to, which can often be a useful tool to connect with people. However, if what they say (to please their audience) differs from what they do, they will generally fail to form deep, trusting relationships due to straying too far from their own integrity.

Adapting yourself to the group you are with is an astute social skill. Just don't forget that it all has to be connected and based on who you authentically are.

PLAYING TO STRENGTHS

Much loathing is felt as dreaded annual performance reviews loom, essentially because – in their current form in many businesses – they are an arena for well-meant but biased reviews. They are also delivered by managers with inadequate training, and most of the content is orientated to employees' weaknesses.

Adept relationship management skills are helpful here:

- Helping each team member develop their own self-awareness
- Thinking through previous work and interactions to identify where the individual is technically and behaviourally strong
- Identifying which of the many aspects of a role make that person feel most enthused and most energised

A leader can then orientate team members to work the majority of time on things they love and excel at, which does wonders for their productivity and happiness.

CHAPTER SUMMARY

It's difficult to see our true selves. Our brains run on overdrive to protect our sense of self-worth, and to create a narrative that shows us as the best version of ourselves. Others don't see us clearly either – they see a version of us, based on their own interpretations, assumptions and values.

To improve how we think, feel and behave, we need to be curious about what we think, feel and do. If we can muster the interest and dedication to explore who we are, free of our own judgement, and also invite others to let us know what they see, then we will have the best opportunity to see the truth. After that, we can choose what we want to do differently.

In this chapter you have seen the myriad aspects of our work lives that are impacted by emotional intelligence:

- Motivation
- Conflict
- Coaching
- Influencing

- Managing our emotions
- Seeing different perspectives
- Adaptability
- The effects of positive emotion, teamwork and inspiring leadership

These form the foundation for creating a happier workplace.

KEY REMINDERS FROM THIS CHAPTER

- The brain behaves instinctually. With practice, though, it can be retrained to embrace different patterns of thoughts and reactions.
- When you feel defensiveness, blame or justification, remember that is natural, but it's also not useful. You can calm your amygdala by noticing and naming how you feel, and by breathing deeply to regain a sense of calm. Once calmer, you can see past defensiveness and glean useful information from what you felt was threatening in the first place.
- When you have experienced an emotional or uncomfortable situation, once the dust has settled, go back and think through it. *What happened? How did I feel? What was I thinking? What did I need?*
- Challenge your perspective. It's not right or wrong – it's just what you think, based on your genes and life experiences. Someone else's perspective is not right or wrong either. You don't have to agree with the other person, and you will develop your empathy and have better relationships if you work hard to step into their perspective.
- Discussing your emotions helps forge connections with colleagues. There's no need to overshare, but when you're experiencing worry, embarrassment, guilt or moments of elation, sharing these emotions with someone is a quintessential aspect of being human.

CHAPTER 3

VISION, PURPOSE AND MEANINGFUL WORK

100 years ago, strategies for motivation were based largely on the stick approach, designed for jobs that were more manual and algorithmic. As our jobs and needs have evolved, so must our techniques to motivate our teams. Efficiency and productivity are great, but they don't always come from turning the screw. In fact, initiatives intended to boost productivity and motivation can often have the opposite effect.

In a well-known quote, Simon Sinek emphasised how people expect a return when they are financially invested, but when they are emotionally invested, they want to contribute. Leaders and employees have the opportunity to unlearn old tenets and tap into the teachings of modern-day psychology. We're now in an era where most people need an emotional connection to what they do in order to do their best work. Some jobs have a more obvious emotional connection to their purpose; for example, doctors, nurses and firefighters fundamentally save lives and help people keep healthy and happy. While many of us might at first struggle to see our jobs as visionary, purposeful and meaningful, we will learn that every job can feel like that. We can all create a narrative that guides us away from thinking and talking about *what* we do, to talking about *why* we do it.

INTRINSIC AND EXTRINSIC MOTIVATORS

In 1973 a group of 51 preschoolers, who all enjoyed drawing, took part in a study devised by psychologist Mark R Lepper and his colleagues, who wanted to test the effectiveness of rewards on children. The preschoolers were randomly split into groups with three different conditions:

- Group 1 children were told that they would be given a reward certificate if they took part.

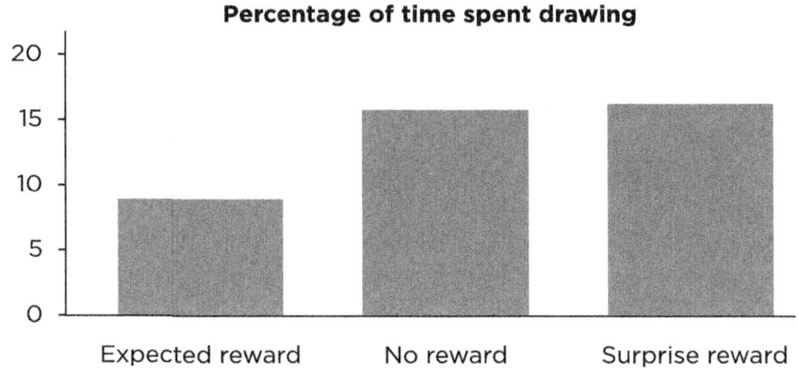

- Group 2 would also receive a certificate, but they were only given this as a surprise after they had taken part.
- Group 3 expected no reward and didn't receive one.

The children were then monitored over several days, and on each day they would draw for six minutes. They would then receive or not receive their reward, depending on the group they were in.

Every child in the experiment had been selected because they particularly liked drawing. The results show that:

- The group who expected a reward drew for the least amount of time.
- The group who received no reward or the surprise reward drew for double the amount of time than those being rewarded for their effort.

The creativity of the children's drawings was also rated, and group 1, who expected a reward, were judged to have produced less aesthetically pleasing drawings than the others.

These results are explained by the difference in *intrinsic* motivation – things we do because we derive enjoyment or pleasure from doing them; and *extrinsic* motivation – things we do because we know we are going to be rewarded for doing them, usually with money or praise. Offering a reward for an enjoyable activity not only diminishes the enjoyment of the task, but it also impacts creativity. By paying people for a task, making it structured and organised, we can strip the enjoyment out of it. Rewarding people for effort, meanwhile, can turn the activity into a chore.

Consider this: if a child likes vegetables but then one day didn't fancy eating them, a typical parental response would be, 'If you eat your vegetables, you can have some pudding'. Simple, enjoyable vegetables have now been turned into a food stuff that requires persuasion and bribery to eat. Offering a reward sends a message about how we should feel about the activity, with the extra motivation signalling that it is unenjoyable.

In the workplace we focus on money as the biggest motivator for employees. Our ideas on boosting productivity or retention therefore invariably focus primarily on financial motivations.

Incentivising teamwork

In 1992 Levi Strauss sought to create a more collaborative environment in one of its manufacturing facilities. Individual employees had previously been rewarded based on the numbers of pairs of jeans they could produce in one day. Concerned by the lack of teamwork this remuneration created, Levi Strauss segregated their employees into teams of between 10 and 35 employees, rewarding them based on each team's results.

Shortly after the introduction of this new reward system, the sheriff's department had to be called to the plant in Tennessee to stop the employees from harming one another. The team-based pay had led to some of the workers doing less because they were happy to collect a reasonable remuneration based on the efforts of others. The employees who came off worst were the top-performing employees, who were earning less than before and were demotivated by receiving less reward.

Trying to foster cooperation through incentive schemes can have the opposite effect to that intended, especially when they are unjustly punitive for some and rewarding for others.

While leaders and consultants debate the relative benefits of different incentive schemes and tweak them accordingly, they may omit to consider that the incentive scheme might be papering over a large cultural crack.

SALARY

Author Daniel Pink, who writes extensively about motivation, puts it succinctly when he says that the best use of money as a motivator is to take the issue of money off the table. Leaders and employees are wise to ensure their remuneration is commensurate with the market and thereafter turn their attention to intrinsic motivations (which we come to shortly), which – importantly – a competitor can't buy with a 3% pay rise.

WHEN EXTRINSIC MOTIVATION IS USEFUL

Studies have shown that extrinsic reward is useful in two particular conditions:

1. Where the jobs being fulfilled are of a more algorithmic nature, i.e., following a preset pattern of work or instructions, which leads to a single conclusion. A job on a factory line is an example of such a job – repeated steps are followed in order for a product to be compiled at the end. Some sales roles also fall into this bracket if there is a step-by-step process, for example in making calls to customers. However, knowledge-based roles – those that require lateral thinking, problem solving and creativity, and where there are multiple possible outcomes of the work – are those where extrinsic motivation can be damaging.

2. For knowledge workers, particularly if we are looking for a surge of activity over a short period of time. Due to hedonic adaptation, which we learned about in Chapter 1, we become used to things, so a shiny, short-term incentive or bonus will eventually lose its shine and will no longer provide extra motivation. There needs to be a careful balance of the benefit of possible short-term boost, versus the long-term effects of a team expecting their work to be continually incentivised to remain motivated.

If we have accepted that extrinsic rewards are effective only in certain situations, let's look at how we can all help cultivate intrinsic motivation, which is deeper-rooted, longer-lasting and altogether more creative.

VISION

The work on vision that my current business, The Condor Collective, has undertaken with businesses and employees has been some of the most penny-dropping and dot-connecting of everything we have delivered. I hope it will do the same for you.

One of the points in our Happiness Survey is *My company has a strong vision.* We ask participants to rate their answer on a five-point scale, from strongly agree through to strongly disagree. Most businesses tend to score highly. But the intriguing part comes from our interview process, where we ask participants to tell us their organisation's vision.

Answers vary significantly:

- Some employees talk of growth.
- Others talk of stability, opportunity or being 'the best' in the marketplace.
- Most refer to goals the company is looking to meet.

We ask this question without denoting what we specifically mean by vision. This is partly because few people ever fully read survey instructions, and also because part of the richness of the analysis is to understand what employees perceive vision to mean in their own company.

Vision: What does the world look like in the future because of what you and your business have done?

Close your eyes and imagine yourself and the world 20 years from now. Look around. What's different? What's better? What problems have you helped to solve? What injustices and challenges have you addressed?

If you can't see anything, you and your leaders haven't yet identified a compelling vision. *Being the best*, or *Becoming a market-leading insurance provider*, for example, is not a compelling vision. It's a goal for winning a competition in which no one is sure of the rules and criteria. It might motivate some, but a compelling vision is about something that people's hearts can connect to rather than only their heads.

Companies need a compelling vision because people derive intrinsic motivation from working towards a better future.

People like a cause. They like living in service to something. They like helping other people. Profit making is important but not compelling for most. Even those who feel strongly about profit being the purpose of their business can create a vision that enables the wider team to connect emotionally with a cause or challenge.

Leaders might find vision a little loose because we are so used to targets being specific and measurable. But when it comes to vision, it doesn't have to be measurable – it's just what you hope the future can be.

Martin Luther King had a vision – a dream, as he called it. It didn't include SMART metrics; it was about working towards rectifying injustices of the past and improving life for people.

The reality, of course, is that our vision is likely to be connected to what we do, as illustrated by some well-known vision statements:

- **IKEA:** To create a better everyday life for many people
- **Nike:** To bring inspiration and innovation to every athlete in the world
- **Google:** To provide access to the world's information in one click

The vision of The Condor Collective is that employment will in future be happier. When talking to our team, clients or suppliers, we talk about our vision of the future before we illustrate what we do. We know that connecting our stakeholders with an emotional connection leads to intrinsic motivation, which leads to happiness, productivity and success.

HOW TO CONCEIVE YOUR OWN VISION

A vision might be social, technological, economic, environmental or political. It is about identifying a challenge associated with your industry, which you connect with and want to help to solve. Think of it as championing a cause and then using your business as a vehicle to do that. It's great for your soul to dream about the difference you can make.

If you are part of a larger organisation, carry out two or three deep discussion sessions with your board members about what each person connects with emotionally in the world or in your industry. You can stimulate discussion by asking others to finish the statement: *Our world/industry would be better if…*

Repeat this process until you can't think of anything further, then compare notes with your colleagues, and you will undoubtedly find some shared passions.

This exercise is also great to do with your company as a whole. Asking your colleagues what they feel the challenges are, what they are passionate about and what they love about your business often provides the raw input to start to craft a deep narrative for what you want to improve in the future.

You may find that your vision statement is similar to others, but that doesn't matter. Your uniqueness lies in your culture, so the way you progress towards your vision will never be identical to another business.

THE POINT OF A PURPOSE

About 20 years ago, a friend told me about an interview he had conducted with a graduate who was looking to work at his investment bank. My friend asked the graduate what he thought the purpose of business was, and the graduate replied that it was about building teams, engaging employees and feeling accomplished. (Cruelly) how we laughed. It was so obvious, wasn't it? The purpose of a business is to make money! That candidate was practically thrown out of the interview with his collaborative tail tucked between his well-meaning legs. I wince now thinking about it.

I was merrily skipping through my career in recruitment reiterating the mantra 'We do recruitment to make money!', and belittling anyone who didn't cross-stitch those words onto a canvass and put it in a frame on their bedroom wall. Success in recruitment is measured by how much money we make, so how could it be possible that this wasn't the purpose of business?

The commonplace fixation on making money as the raison d'être of any business is infiltrating employees' consciousnesses and behaviour from the very day they interview for the job.

> **Businesses need to create revenue and we all need an income, but there is something soulless, grey and unhappy about placing top priority on money making.**

The concept of purpose has grown in popularity in the last decade, largely initiated by Simon Sinek's *Start With Why*. This book presented the idea that employees are inspired by causes they connect with and care deeply about. Rather than thinking about *what* and *how* employees do their jobs, the connection with *why* they do them is infinitely more motivationally powerful.

Purpose: Our reason for existence – the problem we exist to solve.

Despite the concept of purpose now having made its way into many businesses' vernacular, it's still often misunderstood. One common misconception is that purpose is fulfilled if we donate to charities. My first recruitment business always had a philanthropic element to it. Each year we donated a proportion of our profits to charities that were important to our employees and customers, and we invested in training schemes for people in the construction industry. I thought this made it purposeful.

Here is an important distinction. We did something altruistic with our money once we'd made it. It wasn't the reason for making it in the first place.

Making donations was a good thing to do, but I can now see why our employees were talking about it passively rather than passionately – the donations were simply a by-product of what we did anyway, not the essence of why we did it. We still talked primarily about hitting financial targets and making money; the donations were a once-a-year conversation with our accountant. We were not tapping into intrinsic motivation for me or for the team.

If we had instead stated that our purpose was to tackle the skills shortage in construction – and if, crucially, we *believed* in this purpose and lived it throughout our operations and strategy – then making donations to charities to support people into their first jobs would have helped fulfil our purpose. Our employees would probably have still said, 'I'm a recruitment consultant', but they would have probably added, 'for a business that exists to tackle the skills shortage in construction'.

This shift in narrative is possible for every role and industry, though some may need to dig a bit deeper to make those connections.

To start connecting with a compelling purpose for your business, you can start to ask yourself and your team some questions. The process for connecting with vision and purpose is often derived from the same type of questions. However, while your vision is about how you want the future to look, your purpose is framed in the context of why you do what you do. You might start with a question like one of these:

- *Why do you do what you do?*
- *Why did you start the business?*
- *Why do you do it for this company rather than any other?*
- *Why did you join the business?*
- *What has been your favourite day in your role and why?*

Dig past the answers to your first question like *I'm paid to be here* and *It was better than my last company.* Ask *Why?* up to five times, in response to the answers you receive, to elicit information that takes you to the deeper values and principles at play.

Sometimes purpose is sitting right underneath your nose, and you'll find that the slightest reframing or shifting of mindset can connect you with the purpose of your work. We found an example of exactly this when interviewing one of our client's employees.

Nailing the narrative

When interviewing Caroline, we discussed the blend of her employer's values with her own personal values. She said that, since moving to a bigger company, she felt that their values were more commercial than she was used to.

She said, 'Ultimately, construction is about making money. It's a commercial industry, and I'm not sure whether that's where I see myself.'

Her comments became clearer when we compared her current employer with her previous one, which was a deliberately purpose-led business that helped to transform disused spaces in London into inspiring and practical spaces for start-up businesses in the local community.

Her current employer designed and built workspaces for their clients too, so what made that feel more commercial?

It was their *narrative* that was different. Her previous employer spoke about their purpose being to help the community and support small businesses – they talked about what they did differently. They didn't talk about how much profit each project was going to make; they talked about the impact of how their work could help others.

She reflected, 'I hadn't thought about both my jobs being about creating spaces, and reframing it like that is actually going to change my approach to and mindset about what I'm doing now.'

EMBEDDING PURPOSE

When business leaders first started to embrace the concept of purpose, there was a flurry of away days, where management pored over the exact wording of the slogans that would soon adorn their websites. Forgive the cynicism, but – like many other types of new business thinking – purpose is something that many business leaders feel they have mastered once it has been presented on marketing collaterals. An employee isn't motivated by the fact that a business says it exists to fulfil a certain purpose – the business has to *actually* behave in pursuit of that particular purpose. Enhancing happier employment and reaping the ancillary benefit of happy employees goes much deeper than jingles.

When researching this chapter, I sought inspiration from some large UK recruitment businesses and their purposes. Here's what they say:

- **Page Group:** We change lives for people through creating opportunity to reach potential.
- **Robert Walters:** Powering people and organisations to fulfil their unique potential.
- **Hays:** We benefit society by helping people succeed and enabling organisations to thrive – creating opportunities and improving lives.
- **Reed Group:** The purpose of the Reed Group is improving lives through work

These are ambitious, enigmatic statements, and it's clear that these large corporations have evolved to appreciate the potential of purposeful work. It intrigued me to look into if and how they were fulfilling their purpose, but evidence was hard to find. I was left wondering whether even the biggest recruitment market leaders have put purpose at the heart of what they do, or whether purpose is still aspirational or simply misunderstood.

The Forbes article 'Purpose-Driven Companies Evolve Faster Than Others' found that 79% of business leaders believe an organisation's purpose is central to its business success. It's encouraging that such a high proportion of leaders are wise to the concept of intrinsically motivating teams through purposeful work. However, the same study found that 68% said that their company purpose was not used as a guidepost for decision making. The theory is there but the practice isn't. Yet.

Let's not cast aspersions on the businesses listed above; on the contrary, there's much to be admired. But those companies are in influential positions. Smaller businesses will look to them for guidance and inspiration, and they will find that many big businesses' websites are chock-a-block with stunning facts: numbers of offices, how many countries they service, amount of revenue, numbers of staff ... these are the facts put in large, boxed fonts on their About Us pages. But where is their purpose, and how do they live it?

It is time for executives to realise there's more to business than being the leader in an imaginary competition with no collective rules.

In stark contrast to many large corporations' websites, American shoe brand TOMS – a great example of a purpose-led business – puts the word IMPACT front and centre on its home page. Their message is simple: *We believe in a future where all people have a chance to thrive.* Their initial pledge was that for every pair of shoes they sold, they would donate another pair to a child in need. At the time of writing, TOMS have donated in excess of 95 million pairs of shoes. They have now evolved the ways in which they deliver this purpose to restoring people's sight and providing access to safe drinking water.

I was curious about how the TOMS purpose was motivating employees and customers. Their purpose is *socially conscious.* Having shoes is one of life's essentials and – while there is a first-world barefoot revolution starting up – in developing countries, there are over one billion people who have either inadequate footwear or no shoes at all.

Their purpose is *authentic and used.* Every TOMS press release I've seen has their impact pledge in its headline. TOMS was founded in 2006 by Blake Mycoskie, after he had been on a trip to Argentina. He said, 'I knew somewhere in the back of my mind that poor children around the world often went barefoot, but now, for the first time, I saw the real effects of being shoeless: the blisters, the sores, the infections.'

If a purpose is to resonate with a whole business, it's critical that it comes from an authentic leader who has a passionate connection with the purpose.

As Blake Mycoskie says, we know somewhere in the back of our minds that poor children around the world often go without shoes. But many people need to see the problem for themselves to truly understand it. Memories are often inescapable, and once there's a *personal connection* to a problem, people can foster their accountability to help fix it. Many TOMS employees have had the opportunity to see the impact of their work by participating in 'giving trips', where they visit countries to see the impact of giving shoes. Many have blogged about their lifechanging and humbling experiences on these trips, which illustrates how the visibility of the purpose, and the impact a business can have, are fundamental to the motivation of employees.

TOMS customers also feel enriched by knowing they are making a societal impact by buying TOMS shoes, which motivates them to do so. Customers prefer working with businesses that support honourable causes, due at least in part to the feeling that a business that cares about a cause will also care about its customers.

When you are crafting the purpose for your business, ask yourself three questions:

1. Is your purpose socially/environmentally/technologically/politically conscious?
2. Is your purpose authentically engrained?
3. Can you see how you and your team can connect personally to the problem you exist to solve?

A feel-good, societal purpose is not too fluffy or soft for business. It's warm and human. Businesses have in the past often been self-focused, resolute and sometimes soulless for employees. Those businesses that choose to connect with a purpose and live it as their raison d'être will foster engaged, happy employees, because people glean great motivation from living in service to something bigger than themselves. As highlighted by Raj Sisodia in *Firms of Endearment*, purpose-led businesses also outperform the S&P 500 by an impressive 14 times.

Leaders and employees of purpose-led organisations can talk with pride about why their role is important in society and why they believe in the cause they work for. They do their work well because they feel it's important, not only because they are being paid extra incentives to do so. Employees feel more job happiness, which translates to lower levels of absenteeism and job quitting. This is beneficial not only for existing employees but also for recruiting the best talent. Millennials and Generation Z – the generations that prioritise purpose towards the top of their employment wish list – already form the majority of our workforce.

If businesses want to create a competitive advantage for themselves and retain the best employees, they should focus on this emotional connection with their cause. Competitors can offer more money, but if our employees care about what we exist to achieve, extrinsic rewards fade in significance.

Purpose-led organisations inspire this intrinsic motivation, but only if they move past using purpose to dress their windows. To embed a purpose, it has to be used. It has to be referred to in day-to-day conversations, performance reviews, town hall meetings, talking to customers and onboarding new employees. Most important, when making business decisions, leaders must ask themselves every single time: *Is this serving our purpose?* It's a great way to constantly remind everyone of the bigger picture, and it prevents leaders and employees becoming too embroiled in what often transpires to be the insignificant minutiae of employment and running a business. Connecting with something bigger than us helps us to adopt a positive, compassionate and considerate version of ourselves. We need more of that in our work.

SELF-TRANSCENDENCE

In this context, *self-transcendence* is simply about understanding where we fit in humanity and satisfying needs beyond our own. It's about realising that each of us is one small part of a greater whole, and acting accordingly. If we know someone who always strives to look after people less fortunate than themselves, it's likely we've found a good example of self-transcendence.

Reminding ourselves that we are all teeny, tiny parts of the universe is doubtless a good way to keep our egos in check. Older generations will generally have greater self-transcendence than younger people, due largely to increasing awareness of their own mortality. Passing certain landmark birthdays certainly focuses the mind, as we are reminded that we have less and less time do something meaningful for the world.

The hallmarks of self-transcendence include:

- Our own needs are put aside in favour of a service to others
- A shift in values, to being driven by intrinsic rather than extrinsic motivation
- An increase in moral concern – of doing the right thing

This might be starting to sound like a spiritual concept, tuning in to a greater power, but self-transcendence isn't reserved for only the most holy amongst us. I think these qualities lie within almost all of humanity, but we benefit from being reminded to tap into our humility, finetune our desire to help others, and behave with no personal outcome in mind. These are some of the rawest, most unaffected qualities we can have.

We need to have the courage to listen to these qualities, even when they feel like they are being drowned out.

In his TED Talk 'How to buy happiness', Michael Norton controversially proves the notion that money *can* buy happiness. He argues that we're simply spending it on the wrong things.

In his experiment, he and his team gave various Vancouver University students envelopes containing cash, ranging from $5 to $20. Also inside each envelope was one of two versions of instructions: one said that the students were to spend the money on themselves, the other that they had to spend the money on someone else. At the end of the day, the students reported whether they were happier or not. The results revealed that the students invited to spend money on themselves were no happier than before, but those who had spent money on someone else became happier.

Michael tried a similar experiment on a sales team in Belgium, either instructing them to spend money on themselves or, *pro-socially*, on their team. One team member bought a piñata, and the whole team enjoyed thwacking it for ten minutes together. Across the experiment, the results were that the pro-social team enjoyed greater happiness than those who only invested in themselves.

When the experiment was replicated with a sports team, that team outperformed others in the league. Another example is from a Japanese internet company, OzVision, which Frederic Laloux cites in his book *Reinventing Organizations*. OzVision have a cherished practice of storytelling, which aims to foster a spirit of gratitude in the organisation. Each year, an employee is given $200 to spend in any way they want, to thank someone who has made an impression on their lives. The only rule is that the employee must come back and share the story of what they gave as a gift, why they gave it and to whom. This results in employees sharing deeply meaningful moments in their lives, and their colleagues vicariously experiencing the fulfilment of thanking someone who has played such an important role for them. It's a unique insight to gain about a colleague and stimulates an opportunity for authenticity and deep connection in the workplace community.

These experiments and stories epitomise the modern workplace culture we seek: one that exists to create happiness, productivity and success through our experiences with other people. They show how fulfilment actually comes from serving others rather than only ourselves, even when there is a material gain to be made. It's vital to remember the benefits – the feel-good factor in helping others – which is usually a lot more rewarding and fulfilling.

PURPOSE WITH A SMALL P

So far in this chapter we have talked about the purpose of a business being the reason it exists – the problem it aims to solve. This is what author Daniel Pink would describe as *purpose with a capital P*. This Purpose is hugely important but can feel lofty and harder to connect with when we are cracking out a spreadsheet in a basement office at a desk near the toilets. It can also take time for each employee to work out how they connect with the company's Purpose. It is therefore worth exploring how we can improve our happiness by connecting with purpose with a small p, which Daniel Pink differentiates as the motivation we derive from making a contribution. Before we delve more into the motivation we derive from our work feeling meaningful and purposeful, we can remind ourselves first of the importance of a job.

THE IMPORTANCE OF A JOB

> 'Employment is nature's physician and is essential to human happiness.'
> – Galen, Roman physician

Despite the apparently easy option of signing on and living off the state, at the time of writing, around 33 million people in the UK choose to work. Why? What makes people want to offer their time for something or someone else?

The most straightforward answer is that we go to work to earn more money than we'd be given by the state. However, as we've started to learn, this goes much deeper than earning money; otherwise, why would people devote their time to volunteering?

Improving employment is essential because jobs and the feeling of making a contribution are important. They provide structure to the day. They offer the opportunity for people to find belonging and friendships and to keep their world, community and their environment thriving. Jobs offer learning opportunities, intellectual challenge and the ability to gain a sense of achievement. It's also clear that participating in work contributes significantly to positive mental health and wellbeing.

Conversely, unemployment can be disastrous. In addition to reducing a person's income, as Richard Layard wrote in his paper 'Good Jobs and Bad Jobs', unemployment reduces happiness by destroying the self-respect and social relationships provided by work.

Anastacia's story

My childhood was impacted hugely by neglect, abuse, and trauma, and I struggled in school with bullying and an unsettled home life. My mental health was poor, and I attempted suicide. At the age of 16, I fell pregnant with my son and gave birth to him two days after my last GCSE exam. I always wanted to work, but that became more difficult after my son was born and even more so when my son's father left.

When I was 20, my son started school, and I had more of an opportunity to return to work. I secured my first job working as a call centre adviser for the Department for Work and Pensions. I really enjoyed it and got great appraisals from my manager, but the role was temporary and ended after a year. I went back to claiming benefits and struggled to find a new role.

Eventually, I found another call centre role, which boosted my confidence, and I felt things were on the up, but during this time my father passed away from cancer and, as a result, my mental health problems worsened. Due to this, the company decided that they were going to let me go.

I relocated for a new start, and I learned from my adviser at the job centre that there was a four-week work programme available to me that was designed to equip applicants with job specific skills and to help people secure work placements. I attended the course with an unexpected confidence because I think I felt I didn't stand a chance of getting a job with the company – they were a renowned international aerospace and defence company, after all! I was given a work experience role in the company, as a supplier quality engineer. After the scheme ended, I was told that that the company wanted to offer me a subcontractor role. I promptly accepted!

So, I was working for an aerospace company as a quality engineer. I'll not lie – I needed to pinch myself regularly as I couldn't believe someone had taken such a huge chance on me. I was encouraged to apply for an apprenticeship, which I jumped at, and since then I've never looked back. I have moved into a project management role and have gained further qualifications. I now support engineering projects, which to me is crazy because I left school with no STEM GCSEs. Outside of my day job, I am the vice chair and communications lead of the Inspiring Women network employee resource group, an ambassador for the charity Movement to Work and a STEM ambassador.

I still struggle immensely with my mental health. I still have absences from work due to my health, but my company is incredibly supportive and do what they can to help me. I am thoroughly grateful that someone took a chance on me, considering I had nothing to offer on paper. My life is incredibly different as a result. I've managed to buy a house and pass my driving test, and I recently got to take my son on his first holiday abroad too. For the first time in my life, I have a meaningful career in front of me and it genuinely has made a huge difference to how I approach life. I'm also thankful that I can now afford to have carpets and curtains in my home!

I heard Anastacia speak at a conference for the charity Movement to Work, which helps young people into work placement programmes. I asked her to contribute her story for this book because her enthusiasm and gratitude for her job were so infectious. She gives a sobering reminder of how easy it is to take employment for granted and that it is one of life's great privileges. Remembering how important a job is – and that, for some, employment is incredibly hard to come by – is a first step to us all thinking a little bit more gratefully about our own employment.

PUTTING THE MEANING INTO MEANINGFUL WORK

> 'Deprived of meaningful work, men and women lose their reason for existence; they go stark raving mad.'
> – Fyodor Dostoevsky

As early as 1974, American author and broadcaster Studs Terkel wrote in his straightforwardly titled book, *Working*, that employees finding meaning to their work was just as motivating for them as financial recompense. Five decades later, and we still haven't quite reaped the benefits of this insight.

By *meaningful work*, I mean work in which employees can see how their work is important. They can see how their day-to-day activities contribute to the team or department they work in, and they can see how this positively contributes to the grander narrative of their business, their industry or the world. It is about linking employees' work to the overall purpose and vision of the business. This gives employees a sense of significance, which is a vital part of happiness.

Employers may have been slow to recognise the power of meaningful work because meaning is difficult to quantify in revenue terms. In a world where finance directors need an algorithm for revenue results, what numbers could we insert on the spreadsheet for the meaning multiplier? What is meaning worth?

The answer is an estimated US $9,078 per worker per year, according to the 2018 *Harvard Business Review* report '9 Out of 10 People Are Willing to Earn Less Money to Do More-Meaningful Work'. Employees who have meaning to their work are found to work an additional hour per week and take two fewer days' annual leave each year. And not only are they contributing more hours of work, but their hours are also more productive.

> **Considering the cost of meaningful work is zero, there's every reason to work on cultivating it in employment.**

Meaningful work can be fostered free of charge. Whether it's from the societal perspective (that all people should feel they are important) or from a commercial perspective (because meaningful work is worth over $9,000 per worker per year), employees and leaders can start to work on helping everyone's employment feel as important as it truly is.

Many leaders and managers will assure employees that their work is important to the business. Key to meaningful work, though, is that leaders and managers are deliberate in illustrating how each person and each role contributes to the overall purpose and vision, and continuously referencing this in conversation.

> **Such is the importance of meaningful work in happiness and productivity that employees must demand to understand how their work is meaningful. And employers must help them in gaining that understanding.**

The worldwide Covid pandemic offered a fresh perspective on the tacit hierarchy of job importance. Many of us are now so grateful for our Amazon drivers that we feel like inviting them round for a Christmas drink; we greatly appreciate cleaners; and many parents now realise they have no idea how primary school teachers can do what they do on a daily basis. Our perspective shifted completely, and there appears to be a newly instated esteem and dignity for those carrying out these previously 'low-prestige' roles. Rightly so.

A word too for stay-at-home parents. It feels as if those parents self-consciously feel in the shadow of their employed partners or friends. I find it difficult to fathom how this role can lack pride and meaning – if children don't have a caring, nurtured environment, that's the beginning of the end for the human race.

Martin Luther King Jr talked about how our society's survival depends on our appreciation of some of the lower-skilled jobs. He claimed that the person who collects the rubbish is as significant as a doctor – if the rubbish collector didn't fulfil his role effectively, diseases would be rampant. How true.

Author and public speaker Zach Mercurio tells a wonderful story of when he was speaking at a conference for a supply chain management company in Denver. The company made widgets, which were supplied to another company, who used the widgets for a bigger widget, which were then supplied to a company that manufactured medical devices. The business Zach was speaking to had had a miserable quarter of financial results. He describes how he walked into the conference to a flat, disengaged audience.

Halfway through his talk, he stopped, sensing that it was going badly, and asked the audience, 'Why are you here?' Eventually, one woman raised her hand and said that, in 12 years of working for the company, she had never been asked that question. Then she continued to describe how she had only just started to realise why her role was meaningful. She spoke of how she had been diagnosed with cancer the previous month and, when she was in an MRI machine, she noticed that it was a machine that her employer supplied the parts for. She realised in that moment that she had been working for the business for 12 years to help save her own life. The atmosphere in the room changed. It was clear this person's story had given the others in the room – her colleagues – a whole new meaning to their own jobs.

In this example, the woman's role in the business hadn't changed, but her mind-set had, giving her new purpose connected to her company and her work.

You may have also heard the famous story of John F Kennedy's first visit to NASA, in 1961, when he stopped to introduce himself to a janitor. Kennedy asked the janitor what he did at NASA, and the janitor replied, 'I'm helping put a man on the moon.'

A job, a career or a calling

There's a famous parable of three bricklayers who were helping to rebuild St Paul's Cathedral after the Great Fire of London. Christopher Wren, the project's architect, observed the bricklayers on a scaffold and asked them in turn what they were doing.

The first one answered, 'I'm laying bricks.' The second answered, 'I'm building a church.' The third and most productive bricklayer answered with a gleam in his eye, 'I'm building the house of God.'

The responses are often characterised by stating that the first bricklayer has a job, the second has a career, and the third has a calling. Each man is executing the same task, but his subjective experience of how he views the work could not be more different from that of the others.

Thinking of our work as a calling is the type of meaning we can all find in our jobs. This is helped by purposeful and visionary leadership, and by colleagues who consistently reinforce how important each cog is in the wheel.

The exact job that you do within a company can *always* be shown to be of critical importance to the function of a company.

Employers must take care to help employees connect a few steps further than with the immediate, obvious reason for their work. A person's evaluation of their job often depends only on how they look at it, and the meaning that one person derives from their work might be very different from that of their colleagues.

THE TACIT HIERARCHY OF IMPORTANCE

While I worked in recruitment, there was sometimes a culture that those responsible for revenue making were more important than those in support functions. Occasionally, people even uttered the grotesque words 'My revenue pays your salary'. This illicit opinion of status is present in many businesses, and it is harmful.

Have a think about this in your company. Do certain teams think themselves more important than others? For those who have seen this kind of culture, you can ask, *Do we truly think that one person's happiness is more important than another's?* While the esteem of one employee or team may be boosted if they feel more important than another, the esteem and happiness of others will be diminished in the process. No comparison is needed – every employee's role in the business is vital. If it wasn't, it wouldn't exist – companies are not in the habit of hiring superfluous staff.

To connect with how important your role is, it can help to ask yourself what would happen if you didn't do your job. A friend of mine runs a business that specialises in coaching and supporting women returning to leadership roles from maternity leave (and for men returning from parental leave, although this is still a relatively small pool). My friend's background is not in sales, so pitching her business can be tricky for her. She motivates herself every day by connecting with the thought, *If I don't talk to people about what I do, it's possible that women who want to return to work might not do so, and the world would be worse because of that. I need to make this call.*

Similarly, at The Condor Collective, if any of us are feeling jaded or demotivated, we can remind ourselves that every sales call, every meeting, every workshop, every article we write, every interview we conduct and every survey we analyse has the potential of helping to create happier employment. And if we don't do as much as we can and do it as well as we can, we might be inhibiting someone from gaining that happiness. Twee? Maybe. Inspiring? Definitely.

CHAPTER SUMMARY

The ideas and advice in this chapter may feel like a big mindset shift. If you feel that, I urge you to simply pick the bits out that feel within range for the moment. Shifting our mindset to deeply understand and embed vision and purpose is a gradual process.

Vision and purpose are part of the backbone of your business, above goals and strategy. How can we create goals and strategy if we don't know why we're doing what we're doing and what we are trying to change? And why would we expect our team to buy into the goals and strategy unless they understood why what they did was important?

Humans love stories and we love a cause. Crafting a genuine narrative that is threaded through the everyday operations of the business is therefore a powerful motivator and key to employee engagement.

KEY REMINDERS FROM THIS CHAPTER

- We all need money to survive and thrive, but intrinsic motivation – deriving enjoyment or pleasure from the activities themselves – is more powerful. Sometimes, reward for achievements can drive the natural enjoyment out of activities, so be careful of how, and how frequently, you use extrinsic motivation.

- The point of purpose is to ensure there is a compelling narrative for the business and its team. Having a purpose further inspires intrinsic motivation – it is extraordinarily motivating to work in service of something bigger than ourselves. The narrative must be authentic to your business and must be something that people can connect to. It doesn't need to be their personal purpose, but it should resonate with your team.

- To embed purpose and vision, we must actually use it. We must refer to it frequently, we must embed it in our people processes, and we must cite it when making key business decisions and reviewing performance.

- It's easy to become embroiled in the minutiae of work challenges and frustrated when things aren't exactly as we would want them. Taking a few moments to reflect on how fortunate we are to have jobs is a great exercise for regaining perspective and shaping our thoughts more positively.
- For work to feel meaningful, people often need help to understand how they fit into the big picture of a business's success. No one likes to feel their work is futile, so it's imperative that every effort is made to demonstrate how people's work is of the utmost value to an organisation and to its purpose.

CHAPTER 4

CULTURE, VALUES AND ENVIRONMENT

Culture forms naturally in businesses, underpinned by values and shaped by environment. However, without intervention, a culture will continue to morph. A weak culture can become distorted in a multitude of ways. A strong culture is deliberately crafted, and it clarifies and shapes behaviour, rather than behaviour shaping it.

CULTURE

For many companies and employees, culture is amorphous, and we struggle to articulate it accurately. This doesn't, however, prevent us from referencing it whenever discussing employment. Employees cite *good* or *bad* culture to explain why they are happy or unhappy at work. Employers use a hackneyed phrase, *They just don't fit our culture*, to explain why they aren't offering someone a job, or when they are reviewing an employee's performance.

THE CULTURE SUITCASE

> **Culture is a suitcase word – it holds a lot of things inside and only becomes useful when we unpack it.**

Through our research, we have learned that the majority of leaders find it challenging to illustrate exactly what their culture is and how someone does or doesn't 'fit' in their business. One client told me, during an exploratory session about his business, 'People want to work for us because we're … nice'. This was a promising start but was pretty much all he had. The business clearly had a good culture, but the inability to describe it distinctly would hinder them from sustaining that culture as the business grew, and from attracting millennials and Generation Zs, who are more discerning than other generations of company culture.

Business leaders can create a great culture without strategically designing or articulating it, although only up to a point – generally up to around 30 employees. Where leaders are visible and interactive with all employees, the culture can be created by leading by example. A small group of people, communicating frequently – especially when they are physically situated near one another at work – makes it possible to establish quickly which behaviour and practices are acceptable and which are not. As businesses grow, instinctive culture becomes diluted and can morph into a bastardised version of its original self.

In 'Global Human Capital Trends 2016' Deloitte reported that only 12% of companies surveyed believed they understood their own culture. Almost all businesses have a job description outlining an employee's role and responsibilities, and we can be just as meticulous in outlining culture. After all, we don't hire people simply for what they know and are able to do. We hire them for who they are.

> **If business leaders don't understand their culture, how can they create a good one?**

Companies who do culture well, and sustainably, are those who make a point of stating their culture. I don't mean with decals on the meeting room walls, which seems to have been done to excess. I mean that they quantify their culture and use it and refer to it so frequently that it becomes understood.

Culture is frequently gelled into the same sphere as employee engagement but, while the two are intertwined, they are not the same. A company's culture is effectively its personality. Engagement is about how much employees like that personality.

VALUES

This word is now part of the corporate lexicon, and we find values referenced on many company websites and boardroom walls. I find the term *values* confusing, and I think many leaders and employees do too. A better description might be *The stuff that genuinely underpins who we are as a business and how we will behave*, but I'll stick with the short version here.

Values are pretty abstract – they are thoughts or ideas and therefore aren't real. Values become real only if we behave in accordance with them. I could say, for example, that I valued flexibility, but in fact I might behave in an orderly, structured, inflexible way. I could say that I valued equality, but my behaviour might contradict that.

A true value is a principle that our behaviour reinforces almost all of the time.

Enron, the American energy business, went bankrupt in 2001, and several of its top executives were subsequently convicted of fraud. The company was found to have buried losses; deceived shareholders; created a phony energy crisis in order to increase demand for their supply; created complex accounting structures to move liabilities off their balance sheet; and ultimately created a culture by using corruption, greed and deception. Meanwhile, their so-called values – integrity, communication, respect and excellence – were emblazoned on their boardroom wall.

Defining culture

A French recruitment colleague of mine mused that French culture is typically espoused as liberté, égalité, fraternité, whereas he felt a more accurate assessment of French culture was eating, drinking, smoking and complaining.

Not wishing to appear xenophobic, I must add that the same could be said for my home country of Scotland. VisitScotland, the national tourism organisation, promotes the beautiful scenery and lochs, the culture of Rabbie Burns and Robert Louis Stevenson, and historic castles and whisky. I, on the other hand, might suggest that Scotland's culture is actually orientated around deep-fried Mars bars, expertise in pub sports, going commando and playing ear-splittingly awful musical instruments.

Be careful your aspirational culture isn't too far from reality.

MINING FOR VALUES THROUGH BEHAVIOURS

The easiest way to mine for values starts with considering what behaviours are happening in your business. It doesn't matter if the employee count is two or 20,000; this approach will illustrate the reality of your values as a business and will help you stay away from connecting too strongly with aspirational values, i.e., those you'd like to think were true of your business but actually aren't.

A couple of key, easy ways to start to mine for values is to ask a group of people, from different parts of the organisation, to write down a list of behaviours they detest. This exercise serves two purposes:

1. It allows you to align on the behaviours that are most detested, and therefore also on the revered opposites of those behaviours.
2. It provides an excellent exercise in understanding your colleagues and digging into what ticks them off.

The next task is to think about some key decisions you have made in your business, for example:

- Perhaps you had to decide whether or when to launch a particular product.
- If you had to decide whether to let a team member go, what factors about the individual did you take into account?
- If you had to decide whether to continue working with a client or customer, what would the determining factors be?

A client who builds products for the water-treatment sector was going through this exercise, and one of the team cited a decision between two products. One product they were developing used toxic chemicals, which would be fine if disposed of correctly but harmful to the environment if discarded carelessly by the customer. The other product was more expensive to produce and had less profit margin, but it used non-toxic chemicals with no risk of harm. The company has such a strong value around protecting the environment that they made the decision to manufacture the second product. They didn't want to create any products that carried the *possibility* of damaging the environment, even though the responsibility for the safe disposal of the product would no longer have been theirs.

Similarly, a client asked us to analyse a further subdivision of their team and extract the data from their Happiness Survey, as they wanted to look at this part of their business more closely. We undertook all the work and were writing the report, when we discovered that one of the participants' data had not been captured for this new analysis because he had mistakenly put himself in the wrong division. When faced with the decision of proceeding with the information as it was or reanalysing everything with this participant's data included, at a cost of several more hours' work, we decided it would be better to do an excellent job rather than an okay one. One of our values is Just okay is not okay, which was borne partly out of this particular situation.

IDENTIFYING THE MOST IMPORTANT THINGS

Once you have mined for values through behaviours, you can also ask your team the simplest questions:

- *What do we do that is excellent or different from others?*
- *What is most important to us in the way we carry out our work?* The answer might be quality, speed, cost, customer service, communication, perfection, or knowledge (etc).

This list can start large, but it needs to be whittled down by your group. You do not need to mention every single thing you value, out of fear that your employees and customers will otherwise assume you don't think it's important. This is about differentiating your uniqueness as a business, using the principles that you think are *most* defining of you. An example is integrity – so many companies cite it, but do they genuinely behave it all the time? Also, like honesty, integrity should be a given.

You will probably find overlap amongst many of the behaviours and values your group identifies, so you can start to package certain behaviours or topics together. This practice tends to lead to three to five core values. Sticking to these numbers isn't imperative, but if you find you have more, check in on them in a year's time and see which values you aren't genuinely living by and which ones aren't as important.

You may find during this exercise that people have conflicting values; for example, frugality and generosity, or individuality and consistency. When this happens, the likelihood is that neither is a core value for you – perhaps sometimes it works to be frugal and sometimes it works to be generous. If in doubt, you can come back to thinking about important business decisions and consider, *Would we use a value of frugality as part of our decision-making process? Or generosity?* If not, chuck it out. You want to strive to find the most consistent values that the business uses every day.

Values or standards?

In 2015, in my previous business, we did some work on values, and I confess I really didn't get it at the time. I distinctly remember talking endlessly about whether consistency should be a value for us. I felt strongly that it was good business practice to be solid and consistent, so clients and candidates would be guaranteed a certain level of service and to a certain quality. I valued consistency, but I also valued people using their personalities and flair to be different and memorable. It felt conflicting to say that we valued consistency and flair, and I can see now that we could have done one of two things:

1. We could have defined exactly where and when we wanted to be consistent and where and when we wanted to have unique flair.
2. We could have achieved the principle of consistency by embedding it as a *standard* within our business rather than a *value*.

You can make a process standardised, but people can't be standardised, which is why the second approach would have worked better.

USING VALUES

After the buzzy away day, formulating your values and then getting drunk on company expenses, the marketing department are handed the information, the company website is updated, and various collaterals emerge with the values emblazoned on them. Perhaps they might even be chiselled into the marble in your reception area as at Enron, but hopefully you haven't embezzled the funds to be able to afford that.

If we are to create a robust, perceptible culture, which can withstand the challenges of business growth and dilution, can be used as a tool for hiring and performance management, and can be the backbone in an ever changing world, we need to actually use our values.

A great way to craft your values into something usable is to create a narrative behind each one. This is essentially about describing what it means to you, for example:

- Examples of scenarios that the value might be used in
- Behaviours that would demonstrate the value and those that wouldn't
- Short anecdotes or quotes that describe what you mean
- Video clips or film characters that embody this value

This helps to make values come alive. Otherwise, they remain only as static statements on the website.

ENVIRONMENT

Basic needs

In 2009 my business was moving to our first proper office in London Bridge. Despite a tramp peeing at the doorway most mornings, and the interview room being nicknamed the cell by one of my clients, this became a welcome new home for eight of us, all grateful to be moving out of the third-floor room above an audio repair shop in Croydon. We were moving in soon after the new year, and I had arranged for all the necessary connections and comms to be ready for our blast-off on 2 January.

I wept in my car when I found out on 27 December that a supplier error meant we would have no working internet for at least three weeks. Recruitment consultants are impatient people, and I could envisage the faces of my employees falling when I told them that they wouldn't be able to work at full pelt before February. During that agonising wait, we also found out that the mobile phone signal in our office was so bad that we could barely make it through a full conversation with any customer. More weeping. The joyful champagne popping of the first day in our new office quickly dissipated. We managed to forge some pseudo blitz spirit, but it was extremely difficult. Our spirits were finally lifted when we hired a couple of staff from the Snow and Rock shop on London Bridge, to scale our building and install a booster mobile phone aerial on the roof. Once they were back on the ground, I breathed more easily and tore up the amateur liability waiver I'd made the Snow and Rock guys sign in case they didn't survive their mission.

The phone signal improved, and we finally managed to get the internet installed. Our employees, clients and candidates survived the frustration too, but I've never witnessed a starker example of the impact a working environment can have on morale.

Much under the banner of engagement relates to physical elements of culture being satisfied, including the environment we work in and the resources we need to carry out our work. At the time of writing, any company without a skate park, fireman's pole or slide in the office isn't at the cutting edge of creative environments. Most businesses do not have the décor budgets of Google and Facebook, but satisfying the physical motivational needs of employees can be facilitated by creating good thinking and performing spaces, coffee machines, collaborative areas, comfortable seating, bright lighting, etc. This doesn't have to be about gifts and gizmos – it can be as simple as encouraging employees to authenticate their space. A workstation can become an embodiment of its incumbent – a second home of sorts – where people can learn things about an employee simply by walking past their desk. This is about more than just having a family photo on the desk. Being in love with our environment is about making our environment something to love.

Pookey the dog

When visiting a client of mine for the first time, I arrived at the nearest train station then followed my map, looking for a business park or similar. It didn't feel a particularly businessy area, and I soon found myself at the door of a detached house with a Victorian brass doorbell. I was ushered in by a lovely lady who offered to hang up my coat, which she duly did in the cloakroom next to the welly boots and Barbour jackets. I felt slightly confused, not having considered that I could be entering something akin to my grandma's house for a meeting. The wooden floors in the hall were covered by lovely, patterned runner rugs, and a grandfather clock gently ticked away.

'Nigel will be down shortly to take you to the office. Would you like a cup of tea?' the lady offered.

'Yes please,' I replied, hoping the tea might come with a homemade scone.

Office? Perhaps there was some new-build section out in the back garden and I'd just missed the other entrance? Where were the commercial department, the design department, accounts and HR?

Nigel appeared, gave me a warm welcome and guffawed a little about the weather before asking me to follow him to the office. We went through the country-style kitchen, and a stairway at the back led to a room that was undoubtedly the old servants' quarters.

'Come in, come in!' he invited, as he waded over stacks of paper next to a mahogany desk in the corner.

Ummmmm, I thought. This was unusual. In my haste to arrange the meeting, I had failed to qualify the business properly and I could now understand why they were only likely to recruit one employee a year. It would have been doubling the size of the company.

'Do have a seat,' Nigel said, as he moved some more drawings off an antique dining chair in the corner.

It was dark but cosy, and I wondered if we could light the fire in the corner to add to the atmosphere. I gathered my basic information and made an action plan that I would carry out on Nigel's behalf. Then, after wrapping up the meeting, I stood up only to hear a yelp from underneath the desk.

'Oh, don't worry – that's just Pookey. She always sneaks in here to lie on the sheepskin under the desk. She does help to keep my feet warm during winter days!'

And with that I made my exit, amused by the unusual and slightly eccentric meeting. Little did Nigel or I know on that day in 2002 that it wouldn't be long before the millennial generation would actively seek out an employer that allowed them to take their dog to work. Nigel was way ahead of the game.

While he was CEO of Zappos, Tony Hsieh encouraged his employees to authenticate not only their own space but also the whole office, designing murals for conference rooms and competing to create the most fun team environment. Balloons, banners and artwork are pervasive in the otherwise industrial-feel office space. The stoics of typical corporate workplaces may argue that this is fine for creative spaces but not for professional organisations. However, Zappos is an important example to *all* organisations. Traditional industries may be reluctant to decorate an office like a float for samba dancers at the Rio carnival. But even small, personalised representations of who we are will help employees feel at home in their space. We now have more hot desking and hybrid working than ever before, so personalising your space might not be about your desk specifically – making the office a place for personal connection can be achieved in many different ways.

BEYOND THE PHYSICAL ENVIRONMENT

Employees also interpret safety and security differently. For some, these words translate into a feeling of trust; for others, safety might be more literal, especially if they work in a hazardous environment; and security might for others be about whether the business is financially sound.

If employees perceive there to be a threat to their existence, whether that's about collecting income; working safely; or seeing a secure, employed future ahead, they experience an instinctual, emotional response of fight or flight.

Threats to our existence significantly impact commitment and engagement.

Employers must therefore carefully interpret how to meet each employee's physiological and safety motivational needs. The objective is to create an environment to which people feel a strong connection, whether that is about the physical workspace, psychological safety, or providing everyone with a space hopper. Getting it right will create great engagement and happiness. Getting it wrong will result in demotivation or toxicity.

Authenticating our space – in whatever way we can – not only energises employee motivation but also acts as a reminder of how deeply human we all are. This is a lot easier to forget in dispassionate, restrained workplaces, but it's just as essential in conventional professions such as law, accountancy and the civil service.

Reflect on how your organisation's purpose, values and culture translate. Check whether you have the tools to do your job. Ask whether you can personalise your space. Ask whether your job is safe. Ask if you can have a pool table.

CHAPTER SUMMARY

You've probably heard Peter Drucker's quote, 'Culture eats strategy for breakfast'. That's great in itself, but I would suggest tweaking it to 'Cultural strategy eats other strategies for breakfast'. Not quite as catchy, I agree, but it hammers home the point that culture can be as purposefully curated as every other strategy. Services businesses typically spend 60–70% of their costs on employees' salaries. Why wouldn't a business create the same type of strategy for their employee experience as they would for sales, marketing and customer retention?

Great cultures are the single best selling point a company can have, because – different from processes and systems – each culture is unique. Culture is one of the pillars around which a company's decisions, activities, philosophies and practices all revolve. It isn't finite. There isn't a cultural destination to reach, and it's not a corporate Machu Picchu. Culture is more like a perpetual Inca trail, on which we need to bat off any blood-sucking mosquitoes trying to befuddle us along the way. We need to make sure we're always on the best path.

KEY REMINDERS FROM THIS CHAPTER

- Culture is the personality of the business, so not everyone is going to like every part of it. But if your team like most of it, that's a pretty good place to be.
- Engagement is quantifiable – you can find out a score for how much people like the personality of the company. You'll only understand what needs to change in your culture if you ask enough questions, and if your team give you candid answers.
- Defining and articulating your culture becomes increasingly important the greater the size and complexity of your business. Talk about desirable and undesirable behaviours so it is clear to everyone what works and what doesn't work in your business.
- Think about how you can personalise your workplace to create a sense of belonging, connection and safety.

CHAPTER 5

INCLUSION, DIVERSITY AND EQUITY

'I don't like that man. I must get to know him better.'
– Abraham Lincoln

I love this quote because it's so deliberate in its assumption that there is something to like about everyone. The reality is that business relationships are not necessarily about *liking* everyone we work with. It's great if we do, but as adults (especially with a deeper understanding of self-awareness and social awareness) we can recognise each other's differences, respect the wonderful colour that difference brings to our lives, and also reap the cultural, societal and commercial benefits from doing so.

Welcome to inclusion, diversity and equity.

INCLUSION

You've heard the phrase *Charity begins at home*, i.e., that it's important to take care of yourself and your family before you take care of others. This statement is as true of companies as it is of anything else. It's imperative for an organisation to have its house in order before it invites others in.

Getting inclusion right is about creating a culture in which people can be themselves; their different opinions and voices are given equal weight; and there's nothing in the business's attitudes, behaviour or activities that makes anyone feel *excluded.*

We have all at some point been picked last for the sports team, or we have come into a party where we don't know anyone, or we have felt uncomfortable in the group we are in. These situations all lead to feelings of exclusion, and they are uncomfortable.

Vernā Myers, a diversity and inclusion expert, has stated that diversity is being invited to the party, while inclusion is being asked to dance. Inclusion is about no one being left to feel like a lemon at the side of the dance floor.

Businesses that do inclusion well are conscious of their employees building relationships with one another and creating opportunities for friendships. One example is how wide, cross-pollinated connections are encouraged as part of the onboarding process, via buddy schemes and in collaboration and communications initiatives; and inclusive behaviours are recognised and rewarded.

The owner of the first company I worked for understood this well. Despite having more than 300 employees in the business across seven regional offices, he made a beeline to talk to each new person at his earliest opportunity. He greeted each employee by name and picked up with them from previous conversations, for example discussing family or their successes in the business.

> **The effort needed to help people feel included is small, but the impact is significant and long-lasting.**

MAKE AN EFFORT

I did say at the beginning of this chapter that we don't have to like everyone we work with, but it certainly helps. Research we explore further in Chapter 10 shows us that how we feel at work, and the relationships we have with our colleagues, provide the physical and emotional energy that propels us to greater heights. Borrowing Abraham Lincoln's notion again: if we don't like someone, the best thing we can do is to get to know them better.

First impressions

Some years ago, a friend of mine started working for a big fashion magazine, where she found some of the people to be quite different from her. She fairly quickly dismissed some of them as vacant or self-absorbed and happily befriended others who seemed more her kind of person.

> Despite her manager being erratic and overbearing, one of his best ideas was enforcing a weekly team lunch. My friend admitted that, after a few weeks of enforced lunches, she realised she had completely misjudged the one or two 'vacant' team members, and the team was also stronger as a unit. The lunches were also the only time that their manager behaved like a pleasant human being, somehow freed from the caricature of himself he saved for the office. He reverted to form once they got back, but his temporary affability showed my friend that, if we invest enough time and effort, we can understand and hopefully like our colleagues that bit more. In her case, even the boss.

Sometimes the most significant impact can come from the simplest things. I benefit from reminding myself to make an effort as much as the next person. From our work with clients, I can attest to the benefit people feel from their colleagues engaging proactively with them, when perhaps they haven't done so before.

> **Helping people feel included is the responsibility of everyone in a business.**

Leaders and employees who develop relationships with colleagues very different from them are paragons of diversity and inclusion. Rather than seeking out your regular crew of likeminded amigos, seeking out the people most different from us, and those we less frequently work with, is an inclusive duty we can all fulfil. The benefits for camaraderie, closeness, collaboration and communication are infinite.

BELONGING

We all need to belong. Many of us have felt that striking insecurity when we realise we're not where we want to be. I can recall sobering up quickly at 3 am at a new colleague's house, when he and his friends started snorting cocaine. This was not the place for a non-drug-taking, twee Scottish lass who had just arrived in London. They weren't even encouraging my participation – I think they preferred to keep their stash for themselves – but I had absolutely no doubt this was a culture in which I didn't want to belong.

I had the same feeling when I found myself in a meeting with a bunch of litigation lawyers, who were applying for an injunction against me and some colleagues when we left an employer en masse. Even if you haven't done anything to warrant this type of injunction, please believe that it's not a meeting you'd feel you wanted to string out for extra tea and biscuits.

Belonging is about whether we can thrive because we are in an environment where we are relaxed and welcomed, where we feel understood, and where we have great relationships we enjoy. And a thriving employee is engaged and emits positivity to their fellow workers and customers.

Some aspects of engendering belonging are beautifully basic: a cheery hello from colleagues in the morning, or an invitation to join others at lunch, can help another employee feel they are welcome in that same space. However, the workplace is riddled with accounts of employees who spend their first few months feeling estranged and disillusioned because they haven't received common courtesies from their colleagues. An employee in my previous business used to proudly proclaim that he didn't bother learning any new employee's name until they had been there for three months, at which point he decided they *might* be useful to know. Wrapped up in their busy lives, many people overlook the need to be *thoughtful*.

Kindness and humanity need to be reinstated as fundamental behaviour in the workplace, replacing the aggressive egocentricity of the past. This will not only create a virtuous circle of great behaviour; it will also further address the social injustice of exclusion and create more thriving, successful businesses.

Whisky American

After my first year of my degree at university, I wanted a job to tide me over during the summer holiday. During term time, I had been a regular patron at a sports bar in Edinburgh's Haymarket area, a lively student pub owned by a couple of ex-international Scotland rugby players. I imagined serving drinks to hot international sportsmen and waiting for one of them to sweep me off my feet. What I had failed to realise is that when there weren't any students in Edinburgh, this pub was a large, empty, sole-crunchingly boring place to work. I received no training and understood nothing about changing barrels and cleaning the lines. The boredom of the job was exacerbated by the fact that all the other people that worked in the pub, including the manager, either smoked or played the puggies (fruit machines), so while they were all enjoying their favourite pastimes at the quiet times in the pub (all the time), I was left alone behind the bar with no one to talk to.

Eventually, the Edinburgh Festival loomed and the pub thankfully became busier with tourists. I still hadn't received any training, though, so when an American tourist came to the bar and asked for a whisky American, I ignorantly served him a Jack Daniels. He looked at me, incredulous.

'What's that?'

'Jack Daniels. It's an American whisky.'

'I didn't ask for an American whisky, I asked for a whisky American.'

What the hell is the difference?

'Sorry – what is a whisky American?'

'It's a whisky and ginger beer.' (with an impatient, tetchy look)

We didn't have ginger beer, so I served him a ginger ale.

'What's that?' His disdain felt like he thought I'd murdered his entire family.

'We didn't have any ginger beer, so I gave you ginger ale.'

'Jesus! Just give me a damn Jack Daniels then.'

I couldn't help feeling like I had been right all along. As I passed his change back to him, I was shaking so nervously that I dropped a coin into his drink. Of course, I had to pour him a fresh one – another drink he'd never asked for.

Thankfully, he didn't stay for another.

Many of us have had crappy encounters with customers at work, but these are easier to bear when we feel part of the team and have good camaraderie with our colleagues. If our managers and team mates are preoccupied with their own interests, it's difficult to feel we belong. I guess I could have taken up gambling or smoking …

The authentic you

> 'Be yourself. Everyone else is already taken.'
> – Oscar Wilde

These are bold words of encouragement from Oscar Wilde, a man who was prevented from being himself because homosexuality was a crime in the late 19th century. Even without ridiculous, prejudiced legislation, many people struggle to be themselves at work, which is a sad state of affairs for their happiness, not to mention an afront to social justice.

Everyone has a right to happiness, and part of being happy involves speaking freely and feeling welcomed into a group.

For those who have enjoyed the privilege of being accepted with little prejudice throughout their lives, it's difficult to comprehend the mental burden of those who haven't. However, rather than subconsciously lounging in privileged ease, we must constantly ask ourselves:

- *What does this feel like for other people?*
- *What changes could I make that would help them feel a sense of belonging?*

We will then start to fulfil our responsibility for each other's happiness.

Fancy a beer?

A friend of mine wanted to take one of his team out to celebrate some great work he had done. It was only when they sat down in the pub, with two pints in front of them, that my friend suddenly noticed his drinking partner looked a little awkward.

'Sam, are you Muslim?'

'Yes, but I didn't want to be awkward.'

My friend felt saddened that he hadn't already known that Sam was Muslim, and that Sam hadn't felt comfortable enough to say that a trip to the pub wouldn't be that great a treat for him.

Racism and prejudice are thankfully on the decline in the UK, but this is about much more than eradicating overt prejudice and reducing discrimination lawsuits. Even if the obvious stuff is diminishing, there are subtler things that can transform a workplace, from one that *thinks* it has nailed inclusion to one that is actually in bed with it. And the impact is profound.

A female gay friend of mine told me that one of her bugbears at work when meeting new colleagues is that she would often be asked if she was married. When she replied yes, the next question would be, 'What does your husband do?' When she told me this, my heterosexual privilege jumped straight to the question that, given that the majority of people are heterosexual, wasn't it justifiable that they would ask about a husband? Oh, how I didn't get it.

No one wants to feel they are part of a minority, so the majority argument is feeble and inconsiderate. Besides, it's hardly difficult for us to adapt our language to, 'What does your partner do?' In asking the question this way, my friend could answer with ease, 'She is a chef', feeling confident that she worked with inclusive, accepting people and was instantly considered as much a part of the gang as her heterosexual colleagues.

Consider her sense of belonging. Having endured years of feeling she had to hide her sexual orientation, especially in a traditional workplace, how lovely would it be for her to find that employees were using inclusive language?

Feeling we have to conceal parts of our everyday personal life from work colleagues is a burden on mental health, and it's a pressure that many protected groups have had to endure for decades. Only when employees are truly comfortable at work can they form crucial social bonds.

When we talk about being our authentic selves at work, this doesn't necessarily mean we have a free pass to wear a Saturday night out-out outfit, or give our colleagues short shrift, even if we authentically feel like doing that on some days.

> **Leaders can't ask their employees to endure their worst behaviour, and employees can't ask the same of their leaders.**

Managing our emotions and behaviour is an important part of personal growth. In the same way I don't bring the whole of my authentic self to meet my mother-in-law, because she doesn't appreciate swearing as much as I do, the workplace is a place where we adapt our behaviour to be appropriate for our colleagues and company. However, we do want people to feel comfortable when sharing personal information. This might include enabling people to be free of judgement or prejudice around their sexual orientation or the gender they identify with. It could be empowering people to shake off emotional assumptions, for example that crying makes us look weak, getting angry makes us look crazy (particularly if we are female), and speaking up to superiors is to be feared. The examples are endless.

Designing employee engagement should include language and behaviour that supports all employees feeling welcome and unjudged.

Progressive organisations will lead by example, won't tolerate exclusory behaviour or outdated attitudes, and will seek thoughts and opinions from all employees to shape how they can best create a feeling of belonging for everyone.

Archaic, unprogressive leaders might well roll their eyes at the suggestion of adapting language and behaviour for what might be a small minority. They will claim that those who don't like it just need to suck it up. I would challenge those leaders to consciously choose whether they can stand how selfish that sounds, and to ask themselves, *What does it feel like for other people?*

His authentic self

In 2009 I employed a man called Simon, who had the hardest work ethic I have ever witnessed. He would make more phone calls in an hour than many would make in a day.

Simon was also extremely reliable – he was often in the office at 7 am, and he would work solidly until 6 pm or beyond, only stopping for fag breaks and a quick half-hour at lunchtime to roam around Borough Market looking to experiment with another different lunch. Famously adventurous, he never ate the same thing twice.

One morning, in 2012, we all became quite concerned that Simon hadn't appeared in the office by 8 am, which was unheard of for him. By 10 am we had looked up his emergency contact numbers and phoned his mum, who was none the wiser. Then someone mentioned he had been going out the night before, and we grew concerned that he might be lying comatose in a ditch somewhere. I contacted our mobile phone provider to see if we could track him down via his phone location or from calls or texts he had made the evening before. I received the itemised list of calls and messages made on his phone and started dialling them all. Eventually, I reached a woman who confirmed she knew where Simon was, that he was at her house and would be at work shortly. I found it odd, though, that she didn't hand the phone over when I asked to speak to him.

Simon arrived in the office about two hours later and revealed all. His date, with a dominatrix City lawyer, had turned into a prolonged sex session, in which she had fed him Viagra all night and handcuffed him to her bed. She wouldn't let him leave in the morning, and it was my phone call that had persuaded her it might be time to let her captive go. Clearly, she hadn't passed Simon the phone because he wouldn't have been able to put it to his ear with his handcuffed hand.

Simon retained his exemplary work record with us. We thought it admirable that he felt comfortable to regale the whole story to us and that the only thing to stop him getting to work by 7 am was being handcuffed to a dominatrix's bed. And we at least had an idea where we could find him the next time he was late for work.

Having a friend at work

One of my favourite maxims by the brilliant Dr Seuss is where he tells us to be who we are and say what we feel, because anyone who minds how we are doesn't matter, and the people who matter won't mind anyway.

Being true to ourselves is part of the equation of belonging at work. The other part is to forge at least one strong relationship with a co-worker. A large part of the happiness and success we derive from our careers (and from life) depends on the depth of professional and personal relationships we create with others.

The majority of employees seek personal connections in their workplace.

Humans have a genetic predisposition to relationships. Other people help us to create fun, laughter and companionship, and while we don't need to interact with people all the time, our socialisation creates a happier, more supported environment.

In 2008 Gallup created a 12-question survey for businesses to assess how engaged their employees were. Their tenth question, *Do you have a best friend at work?*, caused a stir amongst executives and reporters alike. According to Gallup, it's the question that invites the most confusion, and often derision. It's ironic that leaders often question the validity of the tenth question while bonding at company retreats.

'A best friend at work? What is this? High School?' wrote Amy Joyce of The *Washington Post.* Curt Coffman, a global practice leader with Gallup, offered Amy Joyce an example of why best friends at work are so important, as follows. At a manufacturing plant in Texarkana, in Texas, one of the employees confided, 'If the guy that goes walking across the floor not wearing safety goggles is a best buddy of mine, I say, "Get your damn goggles on". If I don't know him, I won't say it.'

Strong relationships with people in the workplace will remove inhibitions and allow people to be confident to do and say what they normally would. In manufacturing or high-risk environments, this will increase safety. In office environments, it will diminish errors and build trusted, innovative workplaces where employees are more productive because they feel they belong.

Work friendships also build resilience – we are more likely to try new things and bounce back from disappointment if we know that someone at work has our back. Being able to share our experiences is cathartic and breeds a feeling of being in this together.

When I was starting my first business, in 2008, I worked for three months at a table in my dining room before moving to the metropolis of Croydon. As soon as I'd hired two new staff members, their presence alone was enough to boost morale. I felt there was something to belong to – some *people* to belong to – and that they needed me as much as I needed them. The fact that we could share experiences with others amplified the great experiences and dumbed down the less favourable ones.

If you watch a reality TV show, you might hear the contestants utter, 'We're not here to make friends. It's nothing personal. This is f**king business' (a quote taken from *The Apprentice*). Yes, there are often high stakes in this type of programme such as modelling contracts, financial rewards or music careers, but it appears many people naively perceive that the route to success is a fiercely independent one. They actively spurn friendships, thinking that relationships are a hindrance rather than a help. Some contestants invariably favour one-upmanship and character assassination as a method of proving themselves. They think they don't need to belong.

There's a noticeable difference in other reality TV series. Take Harry Redknapp on *I'm a Celebrity, Get Me Out of Here*, who seemed to bring his best self to the show. He was authentic; he was loving, openly praising his wife of 50 years; and he was humble, crediting the other contestants for helping him get through the weeks. He soon became the most popular member inside the camp and outside with the public. The relationships Redknapp made over his two weeks in the jungle clearly lifted his spirits, kept up his motivation and made even the toughest experiences bearable. Humbly, he attributes his success to the support of others: 'They're the most lovely people I've ever met, the whole group. There wasn't one person I could ever say one single bad word about. They were amazing. … Without them, I would never have survived. They really have helped me. They pulled me up hills, they've dragged me through the water.'

What do these examples show? In the case of *The Apprentice* – a professional context where a leader selects who succeeds – is it perceived to be more impressive to succeed completely companionless? Is it showing us that some people believe you win by forsaking or suppressing others? How happy could anyone be, trying to succeed that way?

Most tellingly, despite their irrepressible bravado and stupendous claims of self-worth, the most aggressive contestants in *The Apprentice* usually fall early in the process or are retained only to provide cringeworthy voyeuristic pleasure. The winner is almost invariably the person who has been kind and easy-going throughout the series, thereby gaining the most support from fellow contestants as well as the best results in the challenges.

In *I'm a Celebrity, Get Me Out of Here,* is behaviour different because it's under the discerning eye of the public, who are happier when they see people bonding and supporting each other? I have no doubt that Harry Redknapp's success as a football manager was attributable to the deep connections he forged with people in his team. His positivity and praise for each of them, and his humility to see that he couldn't succeed without their support, are qualities we could all emulate for happier employment.

Business is at times an aggressively competitive realm. If we can replace some of the rivalry with social capital – the values, bonds and interpersonal relationships between people that create real value – then we will generate revenues through that formula: happiness = productivity = success.

What truly motivates people are the bonds, loyalty and trust they develop with each other.

Work hard on those relationships. We shouldn't feel that our success will be greater if we try to do it alone or, worse still, by sacrificing or belittling others. If the workplace became less about power and status and more about relationships, support and gratitude, it would be a far more pleasant place to work.

Remember that leaders and employees who develop relationships with people very different from them contribute significantly to happier employment through inclusion and diversity. Let's find out what this investment is worth to our happiness.

DIVERSITY

McKinsey have continued to prove since their first 2015 report, 'Diversity Matters', that there is a correlation between a business's diversity and its financial success. In fact, it demonstrated that businesses with strong diversity are likely to outperform their competitors by 21%. There is also a correlation between diversity and innovation – something every business would benefit from.

'We're not racist – we employ two Black people.'

This was the response I received from one client when I asked a little about their business's diversity statistics. He was proud that he'd cracked 'this diversity thing'. In fact, this provided me with insight into where businesses are – and how far they still have to go – in their understanding of diversity and inclusion. At least business awareness of diversity is increasing: leaders feel pride if they can boast a diversity of employees, and those who lack diversity appear to find that increasingly embarrassing. There are significantly more raised eyebrows these days if we don't have gender or racial diversity on the board.

Businesses have the opportunity for great diversity, but achieving it is mainly down to all employees' belief in its necessity and their devotion to achieving it.

Diversity richness can come from individuals with any of the nine protected characteristics in the Equality Act 2010:

1. Age
2. Disability
3. Gender reassignment
4. Marriage and civil partnership
5. Pregnancy and maternity
6. Race
7. Religion or belief
8. Sex
9. Sexual orientation

It can also come from individuals born in different regions of the country to different levels of socioeconomic status, for example with different types of education, or from different communities and types of family support. The diversity that business leaders are looking for to create a great culture is diversity of *opinions, experiences* and *beliefs*. The culture of inclusion discussed earlier must then be present to create a platform to nourish this diversity.

To understand the impact of diversity, we can look to everyday examples to discover how diversity – or lack thereof – has impacted the way we live our lives. Nearly all consumer devices that track heart rates, such as smartwatches, rely on light being reflected back to the sensor from the blood flow in the wrist. Different manufacturers use different types of light, with many using green light. However, green light is well documented to be more readily absorbed by melanin, the skin pigment more prevalent in dark skin. The result? Some smartwatches have been found to be inaccurate in measuring the heartrates of people with black or brown skin. Similarly, soap dispensers in bathrooms have been branded as racist – Black people have found that the same light-reflecting technology failed to reflect off their skin and dispense soap.

Vienna provides another interesting case study. For 30 years, the Austrian capital city has pioneered gender mainstreaming – the practice of ensuring that men and women are accounted for equally in policy, legislation, and resource allocation. After a photography exhibition in 1991 publicised the lives of eight different people getting around their city, it became obvious that the post-war, male town planners had designed the city for men like them – those going to work by car and mostly at set times. There was no accounting for those moving around the city during the day such as mothers, child carers, the elderly or those with a disability. Through the active engagement of diverse architects, Vienna redesigned the city to cater for more diverse needs. This included widening pavements for prams, and placing more benches around the city so the elderly could rest – perhaps making the difference between them choosing to go out or to stay at home. There were more open spaces, better lighting to help people feel safer, areas for sports popular with males and females, and lifts placed in locations next to stairs.

Our world is peppered with the fallout of homogeny, and we barely even notice. We don't expect town planners and soap-dispenser manufacturers to think of everything, but it's difficult to cater for requirements we don't know about. Lack of diversity within the teams creating, designing and testing products and services means that the experience for underrepresented groups is often compromised. And the world works less well for many because of it.

UNCONSCIOUS BIAS

In part, the fault for a lack of diversity lies with unconscious bias. For example, every business leader has interviewed someone and thought, I like them – they're just like me, thereby increasing the person's chances of selection. Humans naturally like finding things in which they can relate to each other, for example if they are from the same town or county, support the same football team or have had similar life experiences.

Unconscious biases include social stereotypes about people or groups of people, which individuals form outside their own conscious awareness. These have evolved from when we were all cavemen and learning instinctively how to stay alive. Everyone has unconscious biases because we're hardwired to make quick judgements based on information or experiences. If something is familiar, it feels safer.

Call of duty

Organisations love it when employees refer friends to the business. Not only is it a positive endorsement for the business, but there's also an increased chance that the new recruit will be better engaged in the organisation if they have a good friend there. However, we must be aware of the halo bias we can automatically attribute to someone who's been recommended to us, as this can turn out to be a false economy.

While interviewing Jeff, I remembered that he was a referral from Max, one of our existing employees. Jeff performed reasonably well in the interview, but the halo bias did probably tip him just over into the possibly-hire category. At the end of the interview, I started asking him how he knew Max.

'Call of duty,' he said in his thick, south east London accent.

'Pardon?' I had no idea what he was talking about.

'Call of duty. I met Max for the first time in reception just now.'

I suddenly realised that good old Max had referred an acquaintance he had only heard of over a headset while playing computer games. It was hardly the resounding prequalification we asked for from our employees, which reneged any remnants of enthusiasm for Jeff's application. Thankfully, most other employees understood that, to receive their referral bonus, they didn't need to be best buddies, but they at least had to have actually laid eyes on a person before endorsing them.

When we hear about bias, we often automatically think about race or gender, but bias can be positive or negative about absolutely anything; for example, unconscious bias around people from a different region, bias around overweight (or skinny) people or bias against (or for) people who like Coldplay. Buster Benson and John Manoogian organised 175 known biases into The Cognitive Bias Codex, which is fascinating. You can google it to see how many weird and wonderful things your mind is doing without you having any idea. Some more common examples from the workplace are explained below.

Halo bias

This is the tendency for positive impressions of a person to reflect positively on or influence judgements and opinions in other areas. Put simply, the halo bias is when we see someone as being generally better in all tasks because of only one trait or instance.

Horns bias

This is when the perception of an individual is unfairly influenced by a single negative trait. For example, if an individual uses a particular phrase we don't like, we may subsequently begin unfairly judging other things they say and do.

Bandwagon effect

When lots of people believe something, it contributes to our belief that it is true. A Mark Twain quote rings true: 'Whenever you find yourself on the side of the majority, it is time to pause and reflect.' Simply because the majority believe something to be true or correct, that doesn't make it automatically right. Rather, it is surrendering to our human need to live in herds and our dislike of being nonconformist.

The Dunning–Kruger effect

This is a cognitive bias whereby people have a tendency to overestimate their own abilities. It can contribute significantly to employment unhappiness, because performance reviews may be disappointing.

Confirmation bias

This is about our tendency to search for, interpret, favour and recall information in ways that confirm or support our own prior beliefs or values. It's natural for people to unconsciously select information that supports their views and ignore non-supportive information.

Idiosyncratic rater bias

Research has shown that managers highly evaluate skills in others that they are not good at and, conversely, rate skills that they are good at more fastidiously. A review is therefore often more of a reflection of the skills and attributes of the manager rather than of the employee.

The effect of bias

In one of our Happiness Surveys we carried out for a client, we noticed a disparity between the experiences of two different departments. One felt there was a culture where it was okay to make mistakes, whereas the other department strongly believed the opposite.

During the interview process, we had a chance to probe this question further. We ascertained that the employees felt the business owner valued the work of the operations department more highly than that of the sales department. It also appeared to the sales team that the owner was kinder to the operations team, leaving the sales team feeling like the poor brother. Due to employees witnessing this favouritism by the business owner, a culture formed where the sales team became less respected and less valued by everyone, and a rift developed between the teams.

The business owner had no idea one department felt more valued than another. It was unconscious bias at work – an idiosyncratic rater bias, to be specific – where he rated the performance of the sales department more harshly because he himself was a salesperson.

Think about how many great ideas organisations might be losing out on because of horns bias. And consider whether your own hiring managers may have considered a job applicant preferentially because of one thing they said, i.e., due to halo bias.

We all have biases to a greater or lesser degree, but we should all do everything we can to become consciously aware of and move away from them.

Unfair play

One business leader we worked with was renowned for having favourites. These lucky few would be cherry-picked from the droves of other competent individuals, usually for their enthusiasm, their agreeability and their newness to the business – they hadn't yet had a chance to do anything wrong. Their achievements would be headlined, their careers and opportunities were better supported, and the leader would simply be more positive and complimentary to them than to others.

That was until the shininess faded and the leader began to notice that their favourite person was as fallible as the rest of us. Sometimes this would take months, sometimes years, especially if the favourite was an expert in a discipline in which the leader was less knowledgeable. Over time, the favourite would dwindle from the heady heights of a celestial being and would come under excessive scrutiny – something of a reparation for all the charm that had preceded.

The effect? The favourites may have enjoyed their superlative status for a while, but this treatment also generated a level of expectation from their peers, which caused discomfort and anxiety. The feeling of falling from grace in the workplace is akin to being celebrated as the top striker and then finding yourself on the bench, when you are still scoring just as many goals. The non-favourite employees would also resent the favouriting behaviour – it would lead to disrespect for the leader. Any guardian should love all of their charges equally, or at least behave as though they do.

This leader was in fact fairly conscious of this behaviour, as it had been repeatedly pointed out to him, but he didn't understand what was wrong with it. He felt it was part of his role as a leader to invest more time in potential superstars.

Backing people with great potential is often a smart move, but if halo bias or idiosyncratic rater bias are present, and there are no objective measurements or consistent criteria to evaluate who has the best potential, then it's only a short hop to homogeny and disengagement.

Our thoughts and decisions are influenced without even realising it. We are therefore all unconsciously creating a culture of people who think, act and behave in the same way as we do.

Diversity needs to be *deliberate*, in direct contrast to the ways in which we have been unintentionally non-diverse in the past.

While bias is inherently part of human nature, the more conscious leaders and employees can be about their biases and judgements, the fairer and more objective the workplace can become.

THE PERILS OF HOMOGENY

Matthew Syed offers a great insight into the disadvantage of homogenous groups in his book Rebel Ideas: The Power of Diverse Thinking, where he states that homogenous groups don't only underperform, but they also do so in predictable ways. He says that, when we are surrounded by people similar to us, we are not only likely to share their blind spots but also to reinforce them. When those people mirror our own picture of reality, we become more confident in poor, incomplete or wrong judgements.

The Windmill Club

I once heard about a business owner who had asked his events manager to arrange a party for the formal launch of his business. He asked her to check out a few venues, including the Windmill Club in London as an option. For anyone who isn't familiar, this was a strip club, which has since been reborn as The Windmill International.

The business owner had a vision of handing out tickets for lap dances to his clients when they arrived. He intended to organise a charity raffle too, so that guests could innocently explain to their partners that any money they were spending was all in the spirit of philanthropy.

The idea gathered momentum, predominantly because it had been discussed exclusively between a couple of friends and clients of the same demographic. Everyone had reinforced each other's beliefs that this would be a great success – an event that would attract tonnes of clients from the construction industry (sorry – not my stereotyping).

On the day the events manager was due to book the venue, she mentioned the event in passing to another female member of the management team. Incensed by the idea that the business could support such a degrading, misogynistic and unprofessional event, she called an immediate meeting. Thankfully, she convinced the business owner that everyone outside of their demographic – and many within it – would find the event abhorrent.

Fortunately, the event was moved to a more salubrious venue, with a performance by a perfectly respectable belly dancer.

This story illustrates how it's easy to go down a rabbit hole without diversity of thought. If we stick to convincing ourselves that we're following a great idea, with the full agreement of only likeminded people, we might in fact be about to commit the equivalent of professional suicide in a strip club.

Leaders frequently need to make difficult decisions, and those decisions are often not reached in fully democratic ways. There is huge benefit in creating a culture where different opinions and experiences are embraced before decisions are made.

Leaders can help to create a diverse and inclusive environment for decision making if they:

- Invite diverse people to the party
- Invite people from different areas and levels of the organisation who will be impacted by the decision, including those with expertise on the subject matter.
- Are genuinely curious about other perspectives
- *Really* listen to what others have to say, and abandon the terms 'right' and 'wrong'.
- Speak last, if at all

A leader's role is to ask coaching-style questions, i.e., questions designed to help understanding, not to sway opinions or offer their own thoughts. The minute a HIPPO (highest-paid person's opinion) comes to the fore, new ideas tend to diminish, and it becomes an exercise in supporting the HIPPO.

Leaders need to put their egos down and resist temptation to demonstrate their knowledge, prowess or expertise on the subject being discussed. Even if we think we have the best idea in the room, we won't know that for sure if we don't hear what others have to say.

Employees can also help create a diverse and inclusive environment by:

- Asking to be involved in decision making on particular topics of interest
- Leaders often invite participation from interested parties. If they don't, can you speak up and challenge them?
- Considering strength in numbers

- If you or a colleague don't feel decision making reflects diversity of opinion, support each other to form a group to approach your leadership. It is as likely that an introvert might have an amazing idea as an extrovert. By supporting each other, you can do more to ensure everyone is heard.

Bring unconscious bias and homogeny into your consciousness. It's the first step to reducing it.

EQUITY

It's not fair! is a phrase that every child shrieks a few times a day or week, causing their parents to reconsider sweetie consumption, pudding size and toy distribution. Parents usually pander to this response because a child interprets fairness as *equal,* which parents accept and reinforce. That is, until the child asks in a cosseted way why they didn't get as much food as an adult or as many Christmas gifts as other children. Then the parent suddenly introduces the concept that there are children in the world who lack food, toys, education and clean water, and how we should all be bloody grateful for what we have. The children repent slightly, but they'll still keep counting everyone's sweets.

In the workplace, equality, comparison and fairness are often cited as reasons for employees being disgruntled

She got a bigger pay rise than I did.

He got a better company car.

She has an easier project to work on.

He has better clients than me.

As adults, we understand injustices in the world, yet we lose this perspective often in our own insular place at work.

Fairness is a subjective concept, and employers will tie themselves in knots advocating a culture of complete fairness. I don't believe fairness is achievable in complex settings. Instead, employers should talk openly about equity rather than equality.

Equality is treating people the same, regardless of need.

Equity is treating people differently depending on need.

When we look at these images, it brings home the stark reality that many people are given a bike that's not suitable for them.

In a 1967 interview, Martin Luther King Jnr described how, when America freed the slaves in 1863 through the Emancipation Proclamation of Abraham Lincoln, they were given no land with which they could set up their lives. All the while, America was offering White people from Europe millions of acres of land in the west and the Midwest, creating an economic base for their prosperity. Americans would then criticise the emancipated slaves for their inability to create a prosperous life for themselves. Martin Luther King Jnr stated that it's cruel to tell a bootless man that he ought to lift himself by his own bootstraps.

Equity is about fairness based on need.

Sometimes, it's timing that makes things feel unfair. What if a fantastic new parental leave policy has been introduced at work, which applies to those who are starting parental leave after 1 January, but you don't qualify because your parental leave started in December? What if you took parental leave a year ago and struggled by on statutory pay and a limited income? *Why should others benefit more now?*

These situations happen frequently in the workplace and can easily cause employees to feel aggrieved or disappointed, but that doesn't mean they are subject to injustices. If we contest the changes, we're saying we don't think it's okay for something to be improved for someone else.

At work we need to focus effort on rectifying real injustices, which involves separating these from things that are just the rub of the green. When it's not an injustice, perhaps we should be grateful we have the chance to play golf. We'll feel a lot happier for it.

CHAPTER SUMMARY

Creating an inclusive and diverse culture is a no-brainer. It works for happiness, and it works for profit. As with many things around people, it a gradual process to feel included and build strong relationships. We can create great cultures by developing awareness of what in our culture and behaviour is exclusionary, and by making effort to pull ourselves out of our own comfortable friendships and cliques to bond with others.

KEY REMINDERS FROM THIS CHAPTER

- It feels great when you are in the pack and terrible when you're not. Particular attention should be paid to new starters, and to those who find it less easy to build connections with others to help them create a sense of belonging. If you have popular, welcoming members of your team, how about asking if they would help build a culture of belonging?
- Create belonging with simple micromoves – saying hello, starting a conversation with someone new, forcing team lunches – until people learn to like each other.
- Adjusting our language is a simple step any of us can make to ensure no one feels excluded.
- The infallible leader is a myth. Everyone has doubts and moments of imposter syndrome. We all make silly mistakes and say the wrong thing. When we admit our flaws and occasional gaffs, we let people in; and in turn, they let us in.
- Power and status feel good but can be damaging for relationships. Our success is richer and better if we rise together.

- Unconscious bias is far deeper than we realise. We must learn to question situations and decisions to scan for biases. Our awareness of the presence of bias is key to regulating it.
- Equality is treating everyone the same, regardless of need. Equity is treating people differently depending on need. There's a place for equality and there's a place for equity – we need to be consciously discerning about which is most appropriate to a situation.

CHAPTER 6

ENGAGEMENT

My husband proposed to me in 2010, while we were on holiday in Kenya. We were at a lovely little hotel in a coastal town called Lamu, having just returned from safari. I have to admit that I'd loathed the safari experience, mainly because my only previous experience, on a family holiday when I was nine, had resulted in us nearly being eaten by a pride of lions. After this latest experience, having felt like live bait in a tin-can Jeep for four days, I felt I was owed some luxury. Later, as the waves lapped at the Lamu beach and we swung on a hammock suspended between two palm trees, my now-husband popped the question.

Now, I was heavily laden with cocktails at this point, so it's fair to say that my 'Yes!' came from a place of stupefied love and emotion rather than sound reasoning and logic. It's not that my answer would have been different if I had applied sobriety, the pale light of the day and an appraisal of the pros and the cons, but our engagement was exactly what an engagement should be: emotional.

> **If culture is the personality of an organisation, engagement is the way in which we are emotionally connected and passionate about it. If the personality is wrong for us, we'll find better love elsewhere.**

As Richard Branson once pointed out, employees are more important than customers. If we look after our employees, they will look after our customers.

It's easy to draw parallels between corporate and personal engagement. We feel at our best when:

- We want similar things in life
- We have complete trust in the other party
- That party makes us feel confident and energised by supporting and loving what we do

- We feel an interdependence to do something great together, leaning on each other for inspiration and using our different strengths

Our personal relationships are never free from ups and downs, and our engagement with employers is rarely flawless either. Suggesting that we can reach a corporate Shangri La is as unrealistic as obtaining a personal one. However, we can learn to create happier employment by understanding each other's behaviour and needs better, which is the focus of this chapter.

If our emotional connection to a personality stays strong and is based on trusting, respectful foundations, it will flex through good times and bad. It stands to reason that we will then be less likely to go off looking for a younger, fitter, professional tennis-playing version with new balls and whistles – sorry, *bells* and whistles – too.

Engagement has drawn widespread academic study. The shorthand findings of this research show that the benefits of engaged employees are twofold:

1. The employee will feel happier, carry out their work more productively and demonstrate positive behaviour.

2. The business and its customers will reap benefits. An engaged employee will be more attentive and focused on their customers, which not only leads to better customer retention and satisfaction but will also ultimately add to the business's bottom line.

A key attribute of an engaged worker is that they exhibit engaged behaviour. Bloody obvious, I know, but this is a crucial point to appreciate. The attitude and behaviour of engaged employees is infectious – their positivity, their outlook and the way they carry themselves make others also feel more positive.

Engaged employees are encouraging, confident and upbeat and – most importantly – they are not *disengaged.* This might again seem obvious, but it's vital to remember that disengaged employees can be erratic, unreasonable and defiant, and their attitude affects others too, internally and externally.

Why is it this way? Humans want to connect, we want to belong, and we want to be in tribes. Fundamentally, we want to be happy. In this chapter we will look at some simple, free factors that affect engagement, how they are currently interpreted and managed, and how employers and employees can together build more successful relationships. We might not reach that picture-perfect marriage, but we must learn how to make the experience of being together more sustainably like that of passionate newlyweds, rather than of a cantankerous, resentful couple who are only staying together for the kids.

APPRECIATION

Appreciation is about thanking someone for being the person they are – their attributes, their effort, their character. It could be thanking them for their enthusiasm, punctuality, helpfulness or resilience, and they don't have to have met a specific goal to generate appreciation. Appreciation is the feeling we get when we look at an employee or our team and simply feel grateful that they are with us.

Managers and co-workers can show their appreciation in micromoves, which are often characterised as a dance, where one party takes a small step and the other reciprocates, until they are in a fluid and intuitive movement. Those little moves can be as simple as thanking someone, offering a small token of gratitude, or providing reassurance when things go wrong.

It's important to ensure that these micromoves are reciprocated. One person purposefully showing their appreciation will naturally influence others to do so too, creating a virtuous circle of thankfulness. Employees can motivate their managers with appreciation too – it's important for employees to recognise they're not on a one-way street. If we are to create happier employment, we can safely assume that our managers and leaders need these interactions too.

Showing appreciation for each other also nurtures the attitude of inclusion and people bringing their whole selves to work. The more people hear or see that their personality is valued, the more of it they will feel confident to bring out into the open. Both recognition and appreciation make someone feel good, but appreciation is longer lasting for the employee.

RECOGNITION

> 'Don't worry when you are not recognized, but strive to be worthy of recognition.'
> – Abraham Lincoln

Appreciation and *recognition* are invariably spattered across the results of many company employee engagement surveys. I wonder, though, how frequently employees or employers think about how the terms differ. While they're often used interchangeably, they are two wholly different concepts: appreciation is valuing the person for who they are; recognition is about valuing a past result or achievement.

The one request any young child makes every day is 'Watch me!', before they perform a high-kick jump, bundle through a cartwheel or play 'Hot Cross Buns' on their recorder for the 25th time that day. Children are demonstrating a need that continues throughout our lives: the need for recognition or esteem from others. We want to know we are doing well.

Recognition feels great but rarely lasts as long as appreciation for the recipient. This is because we value praise of our character more than we value praise for individual results or achievements.

In a fascinating study, which Dan Ariely discusses in his TED Talk 'What makes us feel good about our work?', groups of people were given a mundane administrative task. The participants then took their work to an examiner and were paid for their efforts, starting at 30 cents. Once they had completed a page, they were given the option of completing another page for less money. There were three different groups, which received different reactions to their work.

With the first group, the examiner scanned their work, said 'Uh-huh', then put the paper in a pile on the desk. With the second group, the examiner didn't look at the pages and simply put them in a pile on the desk. With the third group, the examiner took the piece of paper from the participant and put it directly into a shredder. The group whose work was scanned and acknowledged with 'Uh-huh' continued with the exercise for the longest, and the group whose work was shredded continued for the least amount of time. Surprisingly, the group whose work was ignored continued only marginally longer than the group whose work was shredded – evidence that ignoring someone's work is almost as bad as shredding it before their eyes.

Ariely concludes that we can easily generate motivation. Even only taking a cursory moment to recognise someone's work makes a difference to them – a lesson that every leader and manager should heed. Think how effective effusive enthusiasm would be versus a simple 'uh-huh'. It is also incredibly easy to crush esteem through complete lack of recognition, and the fact that employees are being paid for the work doesn't help.

As adults and employees, we are still saying 'Watch me!', if in a slightly more refined and developed way.

We crave recognition from our peers and managers, and we are looking for signs of status, that we have arrived, that we've done well. We must be vigilant about how we go about seeking or achieving this respect, though, as some practices are counterproductive. Those employees who fight tooth and nail to be heard over others in a meeting, or make critical comments as a means for self-promotion, will only create a short-lived feeling of superiority for themselves. They will also miss out on the reputation they truly desire and alienate those around them, thereby lowering their own potential.

Leaders must be careful not to fall into the catacomb of mediocrity, devaluing praise by awarding everyone a participation medal, and they should be aware of what they are recognising. In recruitment I learned that the constant praise and recognition of high commission earners created some narcissistic idiots who felt they were better people simply because they made more money. If we only praise results, we stand the chance of disengaging others.

Employers and employees must work together on this, especially as it's not immediately obvious when recognition is due. More open discussion of positive behaviour and interactions will elevate success to be about the ingredients, not just the cake. And if the cake turns out flat, employees will still feel motivated if it's recognised how much work went into making it.

ESTEEM

As actor Robert Morley once said, the first secret to happiness is the ability to fall in love with ourselves.

Esteem comes in two forms:

1. **Self-esteem** is the feeling we have about ourselves, i.e., whether we fundamentally like ourselves.
2. **Esteem** comes from others – usually in their recognition of our achievements – and is something of an acknowledgement of status amongst peers.

As far back as I can remember, I confused esteem with confidence. The difference is subtle but important. Confidence is how we feel about our abilities, and this will vary depending on the situation. If you generally like yourself and think you are a good person, you have high self-esteem. But that doesn't mean you would feel confident about giving a presentation, for example.

Confidence is a feeling that can come and go, whereas esteem – similar to happiness – is a more consistent, underlying state.

Those with high self-esteem believe in their judgement and are therefore likely to have better interactions and make stronger decisions. The conviction they feel will translate into productive, efficient working practices. Because they don't spend much time deliberating on their own success or performance, those people are also often successful in diverting their attention to helping others. Conversely, those with low self-esteem can feel shrouded in doubt and negativity. They're likely to be defensive and make more mistakes, and their productivity often suffers as a result.

Leaders and colleagues are generally not particularly attuned to the need to satisfy self-esteem. A culture of power play and muscling hierarchy has been accepted as normal in many businesses, and this behaviour can be very subtle. In these cultures, boosting one person's esteem often comes at the expense of someone else's.

The pilot episode of the popular American drama *Grey's Anatomy* gives an amusing example, following the lives of a group of surgical interns on their first day of work. Much of the episode features the fresh-faced interns cowering and responding to every whim of their supervisor, affectionately nicknamed The Nazi. Her onboarding speech epitomises her management style: she insists that they don't bother sucking up to her – she already hates them and that won't change – and assures them that they are grunts from the very bottom of the food chain.

It may be TV drama and a pronounced and deliberate example of how to hammer people's self-esteem, but viewers can relate to this approach.

Self-esteem may not be quelled as obviously as this in some cases, but it may be sacrificed by a well-meaning manager, whose inexperience or lack of understanding leads them to unwittingly reduce self-esteem rather than boosting it. An example is when managers focus feedback on *you* – as in, *your character* – as opposed to on your behaviour or skills, which would be altogether less personalised. Or when say things like, *Stop being so hard on yourself*, or *You just need to let things go*. These phrases are as futile as suggesting to someone incensed with rage that they should calm down.

Remember that we can't simply tell people to have a strong sense of self-worth.

The feeling of self-esteem is intrinsic and can be nurtured if someone feels valued (appreciation and recognition), that they are making progress in their role (mastery), and that they have responsibility and freedom to exercise their judgement and expertise (autonomy). Because those with high self-esteem are more productive and have better interactions with people, organisations and leaders should prioritise self-esteem as a specific objective.

AUTONOMY

A prevalent employee bugbear is that of the autonomy-crushing micromanager. While we all need some guidance, there's little chance of employees feeling fully valued if they have an imposing manager helicoptering above them. Managers often don't consciously micromanage – the practice is so castigated that I doubt many people are happy to own up to it – but micromanagement is still prevalent in most workplaces.

Lack of freedom is one of the primary reasons employees start their own businesses, despite the increased risk and work hours and the initially decreased income. Giving employees freedom allows the feeling of control, which makes them more engaged.

Most of us like making choices. Employees can reflect on whether they are directed only to what is to be achieved, or whether they are also directed to how they should achieve it. The first encourages autonomy – it's outlining a problem that needs to be solved. The second stifles autonomy because the solution is offered too. And a workplace without freedom of choice can feel like a quasi-corporate prison.

Basic psychology applies from the moment we can make cognitive choices. For example, parents have learned the importance of offering choice to their children, to instil a sense of power and control. Even if they are only choosing between a cheese or ham sandwich, the child feels a sense of control and satisfaction from their ability to choose.

Offering employees the freedom to exercise their own judgement and initiative not only bolsters esteem but also increases the opportunity for finding better solutions.

The shoe department

I recall a story from a management consultant, who had been employed by a renowned high street retailer. He described how Tony, the manager of the shoe department, had shown his team the proposed new shoe display and seating layout, according to directions from head office. The consultant asked the employees why they appeared dejected, and they confided in him that the new layout simply wasn't going to help sales in their department. They explained that the art to selling shoes is to get customers to try on three pairs, which makes them statistically more likely to buy one pair. Customers generally don't like sitting right next to each other when trying on shoes, and they also like to have a spare seat next to them for handbags and shopping bags, but this had been made impossible by the new seating plans. The customers were therefore unlikely to try on more than one pair of shoes.

When the store's manager eventually conceded to try the employees' suggested layout, shoe sales increased by 33%.

There are many businesses that do autonomy well. Facebook is one. While many traditional businesses obsess over core working hours, start and finish times and high attendance levels, Facebook prioritises tasks and deliverables over time. They don't track employees' hours, as they don't believe there's much point in anyone working for 40 hours if they can deliver their work in half the time. The employer agrees the work that needs to be completed, and the employee completes the work. The output is more important than the input.

It's well known now that people who work four days per week often achieve as much as they used to in five, with fewer cups of tea, reduced distractions and less screen gazing, because there is a motivation to finish on time and enjoy the day off. People are motivated by having the choice to work how they want to work, whether that's steadily over five days or powering through the same work in four.

Not all businesses will find it possible to offer complete flexibility – some rely on there being a quorum of people working on the same tasks at the same time, for example. However, it is still possible to determine what needs to be done by when, leaving the how up to the employee.

Adapting to a culture that offers increased autonomy may be tough for many managers, especially those with micromanaging tendencies. But enabling employees to flex their freedom and expertise, within a structure or according to standards acceptable for the business, goes a long way to fulfilling employees' need for autonomy.

DISCRETIONARY EFFORT

Whoever came up with the term discretionary effort must have found the driest term for something so emotional. It is the utopia of employee engagement, yet it sounds like something a condescending teacher might say when dishing out a school report. We'll have to wait for something a little catchier, but at least that isn't fundamental to this whole concept.

Discretionary effort at work translates best to the desire for employees to go the extra mile, i.e., they care about their job so much that they will stay late, help others, do more without being asked or offer something extra, all because they care and feel pride in what they do and who they are doing it for. Discretionary effort is the diametric opposite of the attitude of *They don't pay me enough to do that*, or *That's not my job* – phrases that signify disengagement.

There are many engagement attributes that engender discretionary effort: trust, purpose, fun, autonomy, mastery ... each of these will build an increasing level of care. However, the absence of only one of these can have a negative impact on an employee's attitude to their employment and their care for their work.

Lunchbreak

Caroline was a marketing director for a large brand in technology, reporting directly to the UK CEO. While she was on maternity leave with her first child, a new CEO was introduced to the business. When Caroline returned to work, she worked her socks off, as usual. She cared about the company and what they sought to achieve and would go the extra mile for them.

However, she found after a couple of months of full-time working that she needed a little flexibility to make her childcare arrangements work more easily. She petitioned her employer for slight flexibility with her official finishing time, suggesting she could knock half an hour off her lunchbreak each day, enabling her to leave early on Fridays to spend some of the afternoon with her son. A well-meaning HR director copied her in on the response from the CEO, whose only question about the proposal was, 'How will I know that she has taken only half an hour for lunch?'

My friend's exemplary attitude to work instantly dissipated. The care she had for the company suddenly felt hollow. She'd trusted her employers with her livelihood, and they had trusted her with millions of pounds of marketing budgets, yet there was doubt over whether she could be trusted with her lunchbreak.

Employers need to be aware of, value and protect discretionary effort at all costs.

Once lost, it's difficult to rekindle discretionary effort. Employees will still tend to do what's necessary in the course of delivering their work, but they'll be much less willing to go the extra mile.

CHAPTER SUMMARY

As engagement is a measure of how much someone likes a company's personality, we must seek to make the company as appealing as possible in the areas most important to the team.

Leaders have the usual constraints of budgets, resources and time, but as you have seen in this chapter, many aspects that contribute to high engagement are free. It's impossible to create a culture that suits absolutely everyone in every way, so employers must not attempt to satisfy every individual piece of constructive feedback. Rather, they should identify the areas that are falling short for the highest number of people.

Employees too must recognise that, just like a personality, culture is never perfect. Just as you may forgive your partner for not putting their dishes in the dishwasher, so we must look to forgive a business for its imperfections too.

KEY REMINDERS FROM THIS CHAPTER

- Remember the difference between appreciation and recognition. Appreciation is *valuing the person for who they are,* whereas recognition is *valuing a past result or achievement.*

- The majority of people employed in businesses, whether leaders or team members, are adults. They are in relationships, they raise young people, they vote, they make big life decisions, they have mortgages. Let's treat people like adults. Yes, they will mess up sometimes, but who doesn't? If someone messes up frequently, perhaps they're not in the right job and it's simply time to disengage.
- Consider Facebook's model for productivity, measuring output rather than input. Is this model possible in your company? Can you say *what* needs to be done rather than how it needs to be done, and reap the benefits of autonomy and innovation?
- While we want to be treated like adults, we will always have a need, to a greater or lesser degree, for the praise we asked for as children. As esteem is so important for mental health, confidence, productivity and decision making, let's set the bar high for appreciation and recognition in businesses. Could you make it a measurable metric?
- Engagement is about emotional connection, where we flex and move with the natural ups and downs of the world. We don't need to disengage at the first sign of a better offer or after a heated conflict. We can use our emotional intelligence to see situations more clearly, check different perspectives and – with fresh eyes – decide how we feel about our engagement.

CHAPTER 7

GROWTH

In the UK, a typical cycle for an arable farmer starts in September, when the ground is worked and the seeds are sewn. Crops grow rapidly in spring and are harvested in July and August. The growth is planned, rapid and highly rewarding. Farmers also rotate crops so that the ground can replenish nutrients, or they purposefully let fields lie fallow for a season or two.

Please don't be confused – we haven't fallen into an episode of *Countryfile*. Rather, arable farming provides a good mental and visual tool for taking a fresh look at personal growth in the workplace.

Research shows that our income grows most rapidly from the start of our careers until we reach the age of 45, and then plateaus from this point onwards. We nurture ourselves and then harvest the rewards. While financial remuneration might be a rudimentary indicator of growth – that is, growth isn't always about salary – it is the way in which many employees view and track progression. And I think our attitudes to growth and learning in the workplace follow much the same plateauing curve.

This is a problem for workplace happiness. When we enjoy our harvest and plateau, we stop reaping the motivational benefits of mastery – the feeling of getting better at things. This means we can miss out on information, opportunities and new innovations, to anyone who is still in their aggressive growth phase.

We might not be surprised to hear anyone over the age of 40 uttering, *I'm too old to learn anything new*, or *That's the way it has always been done*. This mindset is restrictive – not only for personal growth but also for the growth of others and our organisation.

STRIVE BEYOND COMPETENCE

It is universally accepted that the first days, weeks, months and years of our careers witness the steep curve of us learning and curating our professions. There then comes a point at which we become self-sufficient, independent and confident in our abilities. At this point many of us feel great self-esteem – that we have come of age – a professional bar mitzvah of sorts. What a relief that the hard work is done. However, with the increase in esteem and confidence can come a fear of fallibility.

> **The more expert we feel, the more difficult it is to be vulnerable and fallible about our profession.**

In other contexts, where we haven't created this expectation for ourselves, we are much happier to receive feedback, and we welcome the opportunity to improve. For example, if a tennis coach watched you and your friends play a match and later offered advice on your backhand, you would undoubtedly welcome that advice from a pro. There's no expectation in your own mind that you should already have a great backhand, and you're comfortable with that. After all, tennis is only a hobby for you.

However, when managers offer advice such as how to improve a presentation or sales technique, as experienced professionals we often feel defensive. There are two main reasons for this:

1. Because our status and ego are threatened. Leadership of the past has conditioned us to feel we should look and behave like infallible experts, and expertise means we are beyond coaching, right? (Wrong.)

2. Because delving back into the learning zone can be hard. Inviting observation, feedback and critique involves discomfort, embarrassment and nervousness. Why would we want to put ourselves through this when we are good enough?

This is where we must decide – personally and professionally – whether good enough is enough. And what is the impact on others if we settle for good enough in our professional lives?

Atul Gawande is an accomplished surgeon, who also writes for *The New Yorker.* In his TED Talk he describes how he, rather reluctantly, decided to employ a retired surgeon to observe and coach him, to test what he could learn. Gawande was pleased with his first observed surgery, feeling it was not far short of flawless, yet his coach had written a page of dense notes. The coach pointed out small things such as how Gawande occasionally held his elbow too high, which indicated he wasn't operating in the optimum position; and that the operating light had shifted during the procedure, so he had been working in compromised lighting for a period. Gawande describes how uncomfortable he found the whole process of being observed and coached over the following months, and he noticed there were periods when he would get worse before getting better. But the process made him realise how profoundly important it was to be coached. Gawande's surgery complication rates had been relatively low throughout his professional career. After being observed and coached for a year, he saw those rates fall further.

Gawande goes on to describe how, in conjunction with the World Health Organisation, he and others taught health professionals in India, who were experiencing high mortality rates in infants and mothers, how they could improve. These were professionals who had delivered thousands of babies, often in testing environments where the equipment and hygiene were insufficient. Gawande and his colleagues demonstrated that teaching accomplished professionals about the small changes they could make would have a profound impact on survival rates among babies and mothers.

The notion that learning and growth plateau once we have reached a level of competence is a cultural mindset in most professions. However, we didn't see Serena Williams quitting her training when she had mastered her backhand. Professional athletes don't go solo once they have reached a satisfactory level of competence. Instead, they look for the next opportunity, likely with a new coach who can help take them further forward.

In business we must adopt continuous learning in our culture and behaviour. Not only is it important to harness the happiness and motivation that continued mastery can bring – simply being better at what we do can also have a significant impact on others. We have started to study the science of diversity and inclusion, belonging, emotional intelligence, appreciation, and more, and it is these subjects that offer the opportunity to grow in ways beyond the traditional interpretation of growth. We can master our roles by learning and practising communication, collaboration, vulnerability, trust, leadership and management. The advantage of these subjects is far wider reaching than exclusively studying and practising the technical aspects of our roles. We must decide whether we are comfortable with the level of competence we have, or whether we want to discover our full potential.

THE VEIL OF GROWTH

In my first recruitment business, we were moving forward each year at quite a pace. Our business planning was good, we were ambitious, and we were accomplishing some great work.

At first, I felt like I was growing. I was learning new things, and day-to-day challenges continued to present themselves. Looking back, I recognise my progression was limited by the fact I wasn't *trying* to grow. My learning was insular, and it wasn't purposeful or directed. Instead, it was happening *to me*. And when we treat personal and professional growth as something that happens to us, we are significantly limiting our potential.

Once we reach a level of independent competence in a profession, tackling the day-to-day challenges in our roles often only creates a veil of growth. We think we are growing, but we're really only doing more and more of the same thing. We're not learning to do anything different or differently.

For some, competence is enough. Others will be disappointed to notice after months or years that they haven't really become any more accomplished in their role or in their life. This can be a disengaging realisation. In fact, it was one of the thoughts that led to me selling my first business and doing something new. I had forgotten that it can be exciting and rewarding to learn something new and become good at it. I had neglected to study, practice and master new leadership ideologies, so I was simply doing what I had observed of others in a small sphere around me. I also didn't report to anyone so there was no one to hold me to account for my growth.

I have seen this pattern repeat many times, for employees and leaders, particularly those who have been at a senior level for some time. We underappreciate our need for mastery and growth, we convince ourselves we're growing when we're not, and we don't necessarily know what we want to learn or how to go about it. This is an example of where reaching for the support of mentors or more experienced colleagues can help to shape our ideas for growth.

It takes courage to recognise we are cruising and even more to do something about it. But in being purposeful and deliberate about our growth, we can achieve that feeling of freshness and accomplishment that is so intrinsically motivational. Growth takes effort and can be uncomfortable. It can be even more uncomfortable to feel that others are flying past us.

DON'T LET FIELDS GO FALLOW

The arable metaphor provides an analogy for my final point in explaining why careers plateau: we get out of the habit of growth. Yes, we can have a rest and enjoy harvesting for a while, but to keep progressing towards our true potential, we need to rotate our crops and stimulate ourselves with new growth and learning.

During school, college, university and the first years of our jobs, we habitually learn. We read, we experiment, we practise and we pass exams, reaching learning goals. For most people, once they reach the workplace, learning moves from heavily assisted and prescriptive to more self-directed and self-motivated.

An unhealthy paradigm, which has crept into the workplace, is the expectation that managers and leaders are responsible for leading employees' learning. I have heard many criticisms levied at businesses for failing to set effective learning and development objectives. When I have asked employees about the objectives they have set for themselves, I have been met with blank faces.

Employees with the expectation that companies lead learning and development aren't at fault. Companies have created this expectation by promising training, support and career development. However, this expectation has morphed into the idea that employees, if they choose, can take a back seat and wait to be taken where the company wants them to go. It is rather an insurmountable task for companies to take the lead on every employee's learning and development. Managers are already overburdened, and this is one area where employees can put themselves back in the driving seat and take on the accountability for their own growth.

People need individualised guidance based on their experience level and their stage with the company. Companies should invite these conversations and offer support, but we should take care not to criticise leaders for failing to offer learning opportunities if we have shown little desire to learn.

LEARNING, DEVELOPMENT AND GROWTH

Learning is about gaining knowledge. Development is about applying or practising that knowledge to drive results and reach goals. The outcome of development is growth.

Learning without development doesn't change anything much – we just know more stuff. For example, we could read a lot about politics, but unless we engage in conversation or lively debate with others on the subject, our growth will be limited because we aren't practising using our political knowledge. Growing as a person involves the practice of using what we have learned. Many of us will have attended workshops and presentations, found them inspiring and perhaps taken a lot of notes, only to later file those notes in a drawer and carry on exactly as we did before the workshop. Growth has to be purposeful, it has to involve practice, and it is probably a little uncomfortable.

Imagine the steps involved if you decided to run a marathon. You would need to learn about what training involved; adopt an appropriate diet; complete a build-up of training sessions; and decide on the clothes, hydration and nutrition required on the day. You would then embark on your training regimen, gradually building up distance and pace, sometimes falling back and sometimes feeling more inspired. You would encounter discomfort but push through it, achieving distances you would previously have thought impossible. You would also encounter successes that would motivate you to keep going. You might enlist a coach or expert friend to support you and offer advice. Finally, you would run the marathon. After all those steps, you would also know you'd grown because you would feel the difference in yourself.

REDEFINING GROWTH

Roles predominantly begin with technical expertise, and if we want to progress, we often have to make the decision of whether to become a manager. The pyramid structure of an organisation's hierarchy is so powerful and engrained that management becomes employees' main – or only – career aspiration. We know that some people grow to become wonderful managers, and we know that some are better suited to non-managerial technical roles. Yet the traditional structure of hierarchical businesses, the narrative we place on the prestige of management, and the pay structures that reward managerial roles more advantageously than expert technical roles leave people with little indecision on how they want to progress.

It's this misinterpretation of growth that leaders need to disrupt.

Leadership habitually talks to employees about developing and *going up* in the world. A better analogy is the idea of *going out*. I believe that the ideal career description for any employee is like a messy roadmap, where they stop to refuel and pick up supplies along the way. Refuelling here is about taking stock. Picking up supplies is about collecting tools, skills and behaviour we don't have, all of which helps to finetune the engine as we practise driving. We don't know our final destination when we set out, but we want to enjoy the journey.

The reality is there are plenty of ways to grow, if organisations can see fit to offer them.

Organisations can change the narrative on growth. Development isn't always about promotion to management, and communicating this clearly helps to shape careers and expectations far more fruitfully than the idea of the employment ladder. Organisations must consciously reaffirm that growth and promotion (especially to manager level) are different things and give employees different options. Not everyone should be a leader, and we will start to improve the calibre of managers if we stop making the manager role the only attractive option for growth.

Employees aspire to management because there's nowhere else obvious to go.

If leaders create a culture that values technical experts on the same footing as multi-skilled managers, and if they create an organisational structure of status and reward that reflects this, businesses will have more suitable options to offer to those with a predisposed aptitude for management and to those without.

THE GROWTH MINDSET

The *growth mindset* is the brainchild of Carol Dweck, an American psychologist who was first intrigued by the question of where optimism or pessimism comes from, i.e., whether people are born with one or the other. This question led her to discover that:

- Some people have particularly fixed thoughts about traits and abilities, thinking that everyone is born the way they are.

- Others have a growth mindset, where they believe that, with enough dedication, tuition and persistence, they can fundamentally alter their intelligence or their capability in any subject or skill.

According to Dweck, a belief such as *I'm just rubbish at maths* is not true. Anyone could be great at maths if they worked hard at it. While Dweck's work has received criticism from other scholars, and while I personally still believe in talent being – in part, at least – predisposed, the growth mindset is a great attitude to adopt. Those with a growth mindset appear to enjoy a less stressful life, without the pressure and assumptions that they are naturally talented in some areas, or the negativity from thinking they are useless in others.

Those with a growth mindset are more likely to embrace errors as opportunities to learn rather than judgements on what they should already know.

We no longer need to hold back our potential with our misconstrued beliefs. The way to improve our performance is to adopt the attitude and mindset that we can be great at anything if we *believe* we can improve, if we feel it's *worth* improving, and if we source ideas or coaching on *how* we can improve.

Aside from physical attributes and limitations, everything is trainable. As we saw in the above example, it is first important to adopt the mindset that completing a marathon is possible, even if you haven't been much of a runner so far in life.

Until recently, the workplace has suffered, partly because some people have considered their abilities and intelligence as more limited than they are, and partly because they see their behaviour as *just who they are*. Now we understand that everyone can shape their behaviour, attitudes and abilities, growth becomes a question of whether we're willing to try. We might have scoffed at Generation Zs who have been told they can be anything they want to be, but actually, it's not so far from the truth.

EXPECTATIONS, MEASUREMENT AND GOALS

A further challenge in harnessing the feel-good factor of mastery is that a striking percentage of employees don't actually understand what's expected of them. Considering the fact that job descriptions and specifications can now run to multiple pages, it might surprise you that Gallup's 2015 report 'Obsolete Annual Reviews' shows that only around 50% of employees indicated they had a strong awareness of what was expected of them. That leaves the other half with little or no idea about how they can improve and whether they can pat themselves on the back after a day at work.

> **It is eminently possible to put performance measurables – time, productivity, quality, behaviour, etc – into jobs.**

Every job has something measurable that can tell the employee and employer whether job performance is satisfactory and with which they can track their growth. For example, lawyers are responsible for clocking up billable hours; manufacturing employees have production targets; teachers have exam averages to achieve.

Some organisations miss out on the benefit of this motivation of mastery simply because they haven't articulated how to measure success and what good or great looks like. Measures such as revenue targets, results targets, behavioural guidelines or customer-review scores will enable employees to assess their starting point and track their growth.

In training for a marathon, the ultimate goal is to complete it. To grow to reach our potential at work, it is important we have something to aim at – a goal that will be a marker that growth has been achieved. Achieving goals releases dopamine, a neurotransmitter that motivates us to take productive action, but unless we divide our progress into bite-sized chunks, a large goal can be too distant and intimidating to be motivational. A series of small wins will propel us to greater success. Practising without a bigger goal can feel baseless, and practising without a series of smaller goals is simply too overwhelming.

DELIBERATE PRACTICE

A theory, developed by Swedish psychologist and professor Anders Ericsson and discussed at length by Angela Duckworth in her book Grit, is *deliberate practice.* After studying countless examples from swimming coaches, world-class pianists, spelling bee champions and her own past experience as a maths teacher, Duckworth illustrates that success is based not only on the amount of time spent on a task, which is acknowledged to be a main route to achievement, but also on the *quality* of time spent on a task. Those who achieve significant mastery in their fields largely demonstrate an application to deliberate practice. They find their weakest spots and deliberately practise over and over to improve.

In some contexts, deliberate practice is easy to see. When learning a new piece, most pianists isolate the tricky bars and practise them repeatedly and slowly until their fingers remember the note patterns. They simply couldn't perform the piece in its entirety before separating out the toughest sections and giving those additional, purposeful practice.

In other skills, which require behavioural or cognitive rather than physical training, the requirement for deliberate practice is not as obvious but is equally important. A common assumption is that people we revere as paragons of leadership, knowledge or expertise in their fields have developed their abilities with time and talent. However, *deliberate* practice has almost certainly been key to them becoming consummate experts.

Angela Duckworth is an expert in her field and has delivered many talks and presentations in her time, but it is still fascinating to read in *Grit* how she prepared for her TED Talk. She delivered her practice run via webcam to Chris Anderson, the leader of TED, and his producer, Juliet Blake. At the end, she waited for their effusive praise but instead received frank and rather cutting feedback. She was told she had got lost in scientific jargon and that she had too many slides. The structure of her talk lacked clear understandable examples, and she had effectively told the punchline at the very beginning, stripping the talk of any suspense.

Ouch.

Angela swallowed her pride. She accepted Chris and Juliet knew more about storytelling and that her talk would improve hugely if she took their feedback on board. She refined her talk and then practised it several times in front of her family, who continued the negative feedback: 'Why do you say "Um" all the time? And bite your lip? Don't do that, it's distracting.' By the time she delivered her talk, it was much improved. If you watch it, which I recommend you do, you'll see it is delivered so competently that you can't believe Angela was ever anything but a naturally competent speaker.

People we admire for being great at something have worked super-hard, and in the most deliberate way, to become great. We just don't see their practice runs.

LEARNING ZONES AND LOW-STAKES ISLANDS

Many jobs are pretty exposed. In those moments when we would like to whisper into the phone in a sound-proofed booth so no one could hear us say anything monumentally stupid, we instead find ourselves in the middle of an open-plan office, where at least a handful of people can hear every word we say.

> **Environment undoubtedly affects coachability and confidence, but what if things could be different?**

Eduardo Briceño thinks they can. In his TED Talk 'How to get better at the things you care about', he promotes deliberate practice but also offers the concept that people should be aware of spending time in the *performance zone* and in the *learning zone*. His premise: at the point of two years into a career, we tend to spend the vast majority of our time in the performance zone, where we are executing our job; and spending little time in the learning zone, where we would have the opportunity to practise improving specific skills.

Briceño gives the example of Demosthenes, one of the greatest Greek orators and lawyers, who spent significant time in the learning zone focusing on the component skills that were important for him in his performance zone. He studied his subject matter, but he also recognised that in his role as a lawyer he needed to be persuasive. He therefore studied great speeches and acting to better convince people of his arguments. He practised speaking in front of a mirror and noticed he had a tendency to lift his shoulder when speaking, so he dangled a sword from the ceiling that would spike him each time he did that. He wanted to be able to project his voice so he could be heard within a busy, noisy courtroom, so he practised speaking by the ocean, amidst the sound of crashing waves. These skills were all honed in an environment where mistakes didn't matter (other than to the skin on his shoulder).

Consider a more contemporary example: footballers. They don't only play matches – they attend training and practise specific skills and set plays. They study video replays and receive mental and physical coaching, all of which is time spent in the learning zone. We wouldn't see a footballer trying out a trick for the first time in the Champions League final.

An employee can read, scour the internet, listen to TED Talks and join webinars to deliberately gather information. Once we have acquired information, we must practise our skills in the performance zone to develop those learned skills. But as we noted before, the performance zone is where we feel mistakes actually matter, so it's an undesirable environment to practise underdeveloped skills.

So, how are we going to try new things? How are we going to grow?

Briceño suggests the creation of *low-stakes islands* – places where mistakes have little consequence. Low-stakes islands could be workshops or role plays to practise specific skills; they could be practising incisions on a cadaver; they could be delivering presentations to internal audiences before moving on to external clients.

It's vital to go to these low-stakes islands with a specific skill to practise – an idea of a mini goal or performance level we want to achieve – as anything short of this wouldn't satisfy the criteria of deliberate practice. The process also needs to involve personal reflection on the execution of the task, and inviting feedback from others, to provide the impetus and focus for our next opportunity in the learning zone.

After we have identified the skills, attitudes or behaviour we want to enhance, we need to think about what the learning zone looks like and what our low-stakes island can be, so we can get some practice in the performance zone. It's important to try and recreate the difficulty of the performance zone – for example, with the same exposure, pressure, background volume – but to do so in an environment where there are no actual consequences.

A LEADERSHIP GROWTH PLAN

According to the 2020 figures from the Department for Business, Energy and Industrial Strategy, 99.9% of UK businesses are small or medium-sized enterprises (SMEs) of up to 249 employees. 95% of these are micro businesses, with up to nine employees; and the overwhelming majority of SMEs in the UK are owner-run.

If the majority of SME businesses are owner-run, the employees will not see senior leadership change much, if at all, and therefore two things are undoubtedly happening:

> **These business leaders will be training their staff based on the beliefs, practices and behaviour they have adopted in their own careers.**
>
> **These business leaders are by and large unaccountable for developing their own beliefs and behaviour.**

In my discussions with leaders and managers over the last few years, there have been many who have spoken passionately and enthusiastically about the development plans they have created for their team members. They had created specific goals and strategies to guide and nurture their teams to improve performance. Yet when I ask managers or leaders about their own growth objectives and strategies, I see blank faces. The best I found were general themes such as *I need to become a bit more strategic and less day to day*, or *I need to develop my people skills*. But the specifics that were so present for others were lacking in their own personal strategies.

In particular, the hundreds of thousands of business owners who are formally accountable to no one will risk perpetuating outdated beliefs, behaviour and cultures. This is unless they consciously decide to hold themselves as accountable for their own development as they demand of others. That involves receiving feedback, targeting areas of development, being interested in personal development, being vulnerable, asking for help, being coached, trying new things, meeting new people and attending leadership conferences, and many additional factors.

Leaders having growth objectives and strategies means that when they are training and developing the next generation, they will not be reciting outmoded cultural beliefs, practices and behaviour – they will be at the cutting edge of progressive leadership. Think how great the workplace would be if leaders and managers were vulnerable enough, interested enough and accountable enough to have the same expectations of themselves as they have of others.

If we can start to look up and down our organisations and ask how others are fulfilling their growth, not only might this provide us with inspiration for ourselves, but it will also remind our colleagues and managers that they too need the motivation of growth. When leaders and employees motivate each other to grow, everyone is more fulfilled and the whole workplace improves.

Here is how we grow most effectively:

- Nurture the mindset for growth
- Establish our goals
- Break the objective into granular pieces
- Focus practice specifically on each element
- Push ourselves out of our comfort zone
- Ask someone to observe us and give feedback

CHAPTER SUMMARY

Growth needs an overhaul. In much the same way as we are moving away from outdated management practices, we need to move away from outmoded depictions that growth always means promotion. We need to re-establish a culture of learning, where those who don't believe good enough is good enough can find multiple different ways to grow and benefit the business.

We know from research by Gallup that the majority of employees do not have an innate talent for management. Unless we want to perpetuate the practice of moving people into roles they are not ideally suited for, we must redesign how mastery and organisational structures can play to people's strengths, and identify technical, behavioural and managerial routes for success.

KEY REMINDERS FROM THIS CHAPTER

- Check whether you are afflicted by comfort in competence or by the veil of growth, or whether you are letting your fields go fallow for too long.
- Do you have a plan for growth? Do you have ideas about what you would like to improve or learn more about? If not, reach out to a colleague, manager or mentor and build some ideas.

- Part of growth comes from our mindset – our skills and behaviours are not genetically predisposed. We can learn new skills and new behaviours when we adopt the growth mindset.
- We should alter the time we spend between the performance zone and the learning zone. When learning, we should adopt deliberate practice in low-stakes islands to build our competence and confidence.
- Our improvement in skills or behaviour is better facilitated with a coach – someone who will offer feedback, expertise and encouragement. You are looking for someone to be the equivalent of your spotter at the gym.
- Set goals – little ones and big ones. It's remarkable how rewarding it is to chalk up our achievements.

CHAPTER 8

COMMUNICATION

'The words you speak become the house you live in.'
– Hafiz

In one of his sketches, comedian Michael McIntyre identifies differences between American and British terminology. As he recounts, rather than horse riding, the Americans say, horseback riding, as if there is some element of doubt about where exactly we'd be sitting on the horse. Brits say we put things in the bin, whereas the Americans have a *wastepaper basket*, leaving the question of where other rubbish should go. And Americans reference *eyeglasses* rather than just glasses, again alleviating any confusion about which part of the body the glasses should be placed upon.

Lost in translation

In around 2006, when my brother was dating my now sister-in-law, Katy, we met for a weekend at my parents' house.

Katy was naturally keen to impress the potential in-laws, so she offered to make dinner and rustled up a delicious shepherd's pie. We were effusive with our praise, and my mum commented how homely Katy's dish was.

When Brits say 'homely,' we think cosy, warm fires; big, thick jumpers; and the comfort of rich, unfussy food. Little did we know, and Katy was too polite to mention, that my mum had just called Katy's shepherd's pie *ugly*. Americans have a different translation of homely, and poor South Carolinian Katy sat for the rest of dinner thinking that my mother-in-law was finding passive-aggressive ways of offending her.

Because we can all talk and write to each other, we tend to assume we fully understand communication. When we see the requirement for good communication on job adverts, I think we all mentally tick that box.

The main introductory piece of work conducted by our business is The Happiness Survey. We measure organisations' strength and weakness across 18 different engagement factors, and across several demographics. Communication has appeared as a weakness in every single organisation we have worked with. If communication feels like a strength to so many of us, where do we go wrong?

Communication is a multifaceted, mind-bogglingly complex set of 30+ skills combined under one banner. It involves every aspect of emotional intelligence, organisation, planning and thoughtfulness. This is about the medium, frequency, intonation, words, phrases and order we choose. It's about whether the message feels authentic or staged. It's about the relationship between the people communicating, the environment we are in, gestures, body language, facial expressions and eye contact. It's about the balance of transparency and protection, jargon or clarity, someone's ability to articulate their point or opinion, someone's interest in or irreverence to a subject or person, whether communication is too frequent or not frequent enough, whether it's informative or entertaining, whether it's factual or memorable. It's about the best balance of speaking and listening, inviting comments from others … and the list goes on and on.

A weakness or misinterpretation in any of these areas can lead to poor communication.

The fact that anyone puts their personal interpretation and values on anything they hear, see or read means that a message can be interpreted positively by someone and negatively by another. We could deliver what we consider to be a flawless communication, only to find it is heard and experienced completely differently from how we intended.

Communication is not specific or finite so cannot be learned within months. Only by increasing our awareness of the multitude of complex skills involved, and practising to improve, can we improve our communication skills. Interestingly, both the communicator and the receiver have work to do; the skills lie not only in the delivery but also in how we receive any communication.

Communication is a soft skill that is rarely measured with metrics that hold people accountable. Most telling of all: when communication is poor, we are terrible at communicating about communication, causing somewhat of an impasse!

While all aspects of communication are important to workplace happiness, we focus in this chapter on deliberately practising the formula and content for difficult conversations, as these are what cause so many people to sweat at the brow.

THE LADDER OF INFERENCE

This is a term devised in the 1970s by Chris Argyris to describe how people subconsciously select information from what they read, see or hear; translate it into something that makes sense for them; draw conclusions from the information; and then act on it. These mental gymnastics happen so quickly we generally don't notice they are happening, and as they are processed only in our heads, no one can validate or correct our thought processes against the communicator's original intent.

Unreasonable expectations

I had scheduled an interview with an employee as part of our Happiness Survey process. I dialled into the virtual meeting and waited for five minutes before emailing the employee to let him know I was ready and waiting for him on the call. He joined a couple of minutes later and, to my surprise, didn't apologise for being late. A small point, I admit, but it felt a little disrespectful that he didn't offer an explanation, and I probably offered him a slightly less warm welcome to the meeting.

It dawned on me about an hour later that we had moved to a different booking system for this round of interviews, where the appointments now appeared in my diary 15 minutes before the start time, allowing for preparation time. Whoops. The employee hadn't been late at all. In fact, he'd turned up early, after I told him I was waiting. Perhaps he'd wondered why I didn't thank him for arriving early!

We learned about horns bias as one of our unconscious biases earlier in the book, where we subconsciously form an opinion about someone based on an initial negative interaction. This type of (mis)communication can easily happen between colleagues, which can get in the way of relationships developing fruitfully.

How to avoid the ladder of inference? The principles are similar to those we learned in emotional intelligence:

1. Being aware that we and others are always going to draw meaning from what other people say and do. We naturally use our values, our belief system and our experiences to interpret information, and this serves us very helpfully much of the time.

2. Being aware that our thinking and interpretations are only our own truths leads us to be able to do two further things:

    - Ensuring that others understand our thinking when we are communicating with them

    - Learning to question communications, to challenge our own interpretations and test our assumptions

We are not 'right'. We only think we are, based on our selective data and interpretations. In my example above, imagine I had simply been curious about the employee appearing to turn up late. If I had asked, 'Was the appointment scheduled for 10 am?', I would have learned the facts and avoided discomfort at meeting.

COMMUNICATION INTELLIGENCE

Talking is a large part of many careers, as is listening. The first part we need to develop is noticing what we are saying. We are so accustomed to our own vocabulary, our own intonation, and our own phrases and sayings, that we don't purposefully notice what we are communicating. And, particularly in situations where we feel pressure – even the light social pressure of meeting new people for the first time – many of us are prone to blurting out something weird.

We speak our habitual words without necessarily thinking about the consequences of what they mean. At the end of this chapter are some phrases to adopt and avoid, but a common example is the difference between *I don't care* and *I don't mind*, which might sound identical. But what if the choice was between two pieces of work that had taken someone hours to create? We might mean to say that we don't *mind* which one they choose because both are of equal calibre. However, saying we don't *care* implies that the work or person isn't worthy of care – an entirely different sentiment.

Noticing language is the self-awareness of communication. If we pay more attention to what we say and how we say it, we will start to curate better conversations with others.

THE BEHAVIOUR, NOT THE PERSON

Parents are now encouraged to discipline their children by saying, *That was naughty behaviour* as opposed to *You are naughty*, meaning the behaviour is treated in isolation rather than defining the child's personality. Branding children as good, bad, naughty or nice can affect the way a child perceives themselves in the present and far into the future.

> **Separating the person from the behaviour, particularly when it's a negative behaviour, can help maintain confidence and avoid a self-fulfilling prophecy.**

This parenting style draws easy parallels with the workplace.

She is aggressive.

He is lazy.

She always does that.

They never take responsibility.

Are these similar to statements you have thought or made? Me too. They are common at work, even if not said directly to the individual. They are also almost always inaccurate. Someone may exhibit aggression or laziness, but it is unlikely they are *always* like that or *never* something else. Adding emphasis to make a point is an unhealthy habit, which reinforces bias. The more times we tell ourselves and others that someone is a particular way, the more likely we – and they – are to believe it.

Objectifying behaviours makes them easier to talk about. There's a big difference between a conversation stating, *I found that behaviour aggressive,* and one with the accusation, *You were being aggressive.* Talk about it not you. Suddenly, the conversation is less combative because we're admonishing the behaviour rather than someone's personality and values. We all behave the wrong way at times, but that doesn't define who we are as people.

If someone has a repeated pattern of behaviour, we need to say exactly that: *We have seen a repeated pattern of behaviour,* and *we need to take steps to address it.* We can thereby support people to grow from poor behaviour with deliberate practice and coaching. If the behaviour still doesn't change and is too damaging for the team or business's performance, it might be time to deal with it under performance review.

We need to choose our communication carefully. Communicating about behaviour is constructive; communicating about people being a personification of their worst behaviour can be very destructive.

TIMING

Have you ever been in a performance review or meeting where your leader or manager cites an incident or behaviour that happened more than a month ago? Even if the content of the communication is delivered well, the recipient will wonder why this behaviour has until now been treated as a state secret.

Timely communication is more accurate. Delays distort our memories, both of the facts and of how we felt about them. They also irritate the employee, who can't understand why the feedback hasn't previously been addressed.

Similarly, leaders feel incredulous when the first time they hear from employees about issues or incidents is in their exit interviews. *If there was an issue, why didn't you talk to me about it at the time?* Timely communication is the best way to address issues, before they become distorted, and also so they don't morph into something bigger.

We have learned that there is sense to rationalising our thoughts and having a gap between our emotions and our response. We need that time to breathe. This means we must judge carefully when we, and the party to receive the feedback, have had enough of a gap to formulate emotionally regulated thoughts and therefore when both parties are ready to have the conversation. Just don't wait too long.

The rebuttal to my example above – *Why didn't you talk to me about it at the time?* – could be: *I did; you just didn't listen.* And herein we see George Bernard Shaw's quote coming home to roost: 'The single biggest problem with communication is the illusion that it took place.' This invites an inspection of not only what is *said* but also on *what is heard*. We'll start by focusing on the latter.

CONSCIOUS LISTENING

Listening is the forgotten part of communication, so inclined are we to focus on our own voices over and above those of others. The term *active listening* is prevalent in this context, but I prefer the term *conscious listening*.

Listening is something we do passively. However, considering we spend 70% of our day communicating, and 45% of that time is spent listening, we should probably focus more on improving our listening skills.

Most people assume that listening – unlike the learned skills of reading, writing and speaking – is a natural activity, one requiring minimal effort by anyone without physical impairment. In fact, listening is a complex activity of both physical and emotional skills.

We must address a few challenges that inhibit great listening and learn how to listen more consciously.

JUDGEMENT

We are wired to draw conclusions from conversations before someone has even said something. Our brain makes subconscious decisions about whether the person we are listening to is someone we agree or disagree with. It is in fact possible that Donald Trump has at some point said something I agree with, but I don't know what it is because I have been so busy prejudging everything he says to be idiotic. Before you have your next conversation with your manager, team member, client or supplier, ask yourself whether you are entering the conversation with a prejudgement. Being conscious of prejudice is the first step to minimising it and improving the calibre of our listening.

CAPACITY TO LISTEN

Most people speak at around 140–160 words per minute, and we have the cognitive ability to listen at around 600–800 words per minute. Because we have tonnes of extra capacity for cognitive function when listening, we fill it thinking about anything else that pops into our brain – what we're having for dinner;

something on our to-do list; how blue the sky looks today. We don't need to judge ourselves for drifting off – its natural because our brains are so wonderfully capable! If we develop our ability to notice when we've drifted off, and bring our attention back, we will increase our ability to listen more consciously.

LISTENING LIKE YOUR JOB DEPENDS ON IT

This is because so many jobs genuinely do depend on the quality of your listening skills. My job as a recruitment consultant, for example, depended on my ability to probe for more information, summarise and check my understanding, so that I could relay information accurately to someone else. A doctor must listen intently for the eight minutes they have with you, as the quality of their listening and questioning increases their chances of a successful diagnosis. The police must listen consciously to the information they are being given, and teachers must listen carefully to their students. All employees are obliged to listen like their success depends on it. Because it does. Oh, and put that mobile phone in the drawer.

SUMMARISING

When you have conversed with someone for a few minutes, summarise what you have understood and ask too what the other person understood from the conversation. Summarising the key points of the conversation offers the opportunity for correction and extra details. Don't forget to ask, 'Have I understood that accurately – is there anything I've missed?'

RECEIVING FEEDBACK

As mentioned at the beginning of this chapter, self-awareness and communication are closely intertwined.

The two main reasons why feedback conversations are challenging and often dreaded by both the feedback giver and the feedback receiver are:

1. The feedback is received poorly – we don't handle it well.
2. The feedback is given poorly – often by well-meaning but undertrained managers, leaders and colleagues.

We'll look first at how we can train ourselves to receive feedback better, even if it is delivered poorly.

We must work hard to understand our needs, thoughts and emotions when we are being given feedback – we will hear it more clearly if we are in a balanced emotional state rather than a heightened one. Ask for feedback when you are ready to hear it. Leaders and managers may already be sensitive to this and will judge when they should best offer you feedback. If they're not, ask for some time to gather your thoughts.

> **Remember: communication is best when people are in a good state to hear it.**

ADVICE FOR RECEIVING FEEDBACK

Reactions

Remember that pesky amygdala. It creates an emotional response to threats as well as perceived threats, which is why you might feel clammy even when thinking ahead to feedback or to a performance review meeting. Accept that your amygdala may hijack your emotions and that what you are feeling is an instinctual reaction. Take some deep breaths to try and restore yourself to a feeling of calm. You will have your chance to talk. For now, just listen.

Saying thank you

It might feel like you are saying it through gritted teeth, but it's important for your and others' growth that you appreciate how hard it is to give feedback. Feedback is one of the best learning tools we have available to us, so don't cut it off.

1% truth

Your mind might be racing in overdrive to justify whether the facts are entirely accurate or whether you feel aggrieved. Just relax. Feedback doesn't have to damage your feelings of self-worth. It's a pointer to you of what someone else sees, and this is extremely valuable. There's a saying that there's at least 1% truth in everything. Spend these seconds looking for the truth. It might be that the majority of what you are hearing is not beneficial for your growth, but you will still grow better if you focus on the minimum 1% truth.

Writing it down

You may find the information more useful in a day, a week or a month. Over time, you might devise a narrative around the feedback, so keep notes to ensure the information stays pure. Analyse what could be wrong about it and what could be right – the truth you see might change over time too.

Patterns

If you've heard this feedback before, it's time to do something about it rather than justifying your behaviour to yourself. Other people are letting you know what they need from you.

Getting curious, not defensive

Other people can often see things you can't, so consider what they have seen and you haven't. Ask more: *When does this happen? What's the impact? How can I do better?* When you feel hurt, one of the best ways to tackle it positively is to get complete understanding. It may feel counterintuitive, but by asking further questions, you often dig yourself out of the hurt rather than deeper into it.

We can't control the sophistication with which feedback is given to us, so it's highly likely we will be on the receiving end of poorly crafted feedback many times in our careers. In these situations, a great mindset is simply that of empathy – reminding ourselves of the shoes the other person is in. The person talking to us may not have been trained on how to give good-quality, considerate feedback.

Let's look next at a couple of great techniques for giving feedback. Perhaps you can circulate these to anyone who delivers it poorly to you in the future.

COIN

This structure is best used when we've observed something and would like to offer feedback to correct a behaviour. COIN stands for connection, observation, impact, and next steps. It works as follows:

CONNECTION

Very simply, ask someone if you can give them some feedback. This way you are ensuring that they are in a good mindset to discuss. It is a genuine question, and if the other person says no, it might be best to wait until another time.

OBSERVATION

What did you actually see or hear? Make no assumptions or judgements such as *I think you were …* This needs to be about facts and nothing else. Use dates, times and information for where the behaviour took place and what exactly happened. Remember, this is a statement about the behaviour, not the person, and you should never generalise *(You always …, You never …, etc).*

Examples:

On Tuesday morning you arrived 15 minutes late to the management meeting.

In your conversation with Debbie on Wednesday afternoon, I noticed you interrupted her three times when she was speaking.

Because you are offering facts rather than opinions or judgements, there is little need or capacity for the receiver to dispute the information or to feel judged by it.

IMPACT

Say what the impact of the behaviour was.

Examples:

On Tuesday morning you arrived 15 minutes late to the management meeting. The impact was that we had to delay the start and didn't get to cover an important topic.

In your conversation with Debbie on Wednesday afternoon, I noticed you interrupted her three times when she was speaking. The impact of this was that we didn't get an opportunity to hear her perspective.

NEXT STEPS

State what you would like to happen next time instead.

Examples:

On Tuesday morning you arrived 15 minutes late to the management meeting. The impact was that we had to delay the start and didn't get to cover an important topic. In the future, please allow extra travel time.

In your conversation with Debbie on Wednesday afternoon, I noticed you interrupted her three times when she was speaking. The impact of this was that we didn't get an opportunity to hear her perspective. Next time, please be deliberate in ensuring others have the opportunity to finish speaking.

You might of course be unaware of something in these situations, so you can also ask for more information from the other person. But because you haven't judged their behaviour, instead simply stating what happened, these conversations can run fluidly and without provoking a defensive reaction.

GIRAFFE LANGUAGE

Giraffe language – or *non-violent communication* – was developed by Marshall Rosenberg in the 1960s. Rosenberg believed that most conflicts in the workplace were caused by the ineffective communication of each party's physiological or psychological needs. The practice of non-violent communication avoids evocative, controlling words such as right, wrong, should, ought to, too much or too little, replacing these judgements with expressions of people's needs. Different from COIN, this framework is most useful for when there is an emotional charge in a situation. Explaining how we feel, without blame or accusation, is the bedrock of creating bonds with others.

Giraffe language – so called for the giraffe's high perspective and huge heart – focuses on taking ownership of *our* emotions, without directing those emotions at someone else.

Someone else doesn't make us angry or upset. We do that all by ourselves because one of our needs isn't being met.

The opposite of giraffe language is *jackal language* – a language of moralistic judgements where we blame, criticise or accuse. We see our emotions as being caused by others.

Instead of accusing others of causing our emotions, we simply need to say what we want to happen for to feel different.

Other people aren't responsible for our emotional reactions, so jackal language provokes defensiveness, counterattack and resistance. These responses start a vicious circle and are counterproductive to harmonious working relationships.

Let's look first at practising the first of the two expressions of giraffe language: expressing our own feelings and needs.

Rather than saying, 'I'm upset because *you* …' (jackal language), giraffes would say, 'I'm upset because *I want* …'. This is self-aware and is speaking honestly from the heart to communicate the need we have that isn't being met.

- *I'm upset because you delivered the project to the client late.* (Jackal)
- ***I'm upset because I want to create a great experience for our clients.*** (Giraffe)
- *I'm frustrated because you disrespected me in the meeting.* (Jackal)
- ***I'm frustrated because I wanted to feel respected in the meeting.*** (Giraffe)
- *I'm scared because you were screaming so loudly.* (Jackal)
- ***I'm scared because I need it to be quiet to feel safe.*** (Giraffe)

Note: Giraffe language always places I with I, not I with you.

FORMULA TO SHIFT FROM JACKAL TO GIRAFFE CONVERSATIONS

1. Evaluate the situation or behaviour without judgement

When … [this thing happened]

E.g. *When the client received the project late …*

NB This should simply be a factual, unbiased account of the facts.

2. State how you feel

I feel/felt … [insert emotion]

E.g. *I felt frustrated/sad/hurt/delighted/other …*

Keep this simple, and remember: a thought is not an emotion. *I feel you aren't taking this seriously* is a thought, not an emotion.

3. State what you want/need

… *because I need/want* … [insert need/want]

E.g. … *because I wanted the project to be finished on time.*

This must be about you and your needs, nothing to do with the other person. You are not saying *I'm upset because you didn't finish the project on time*, because that would be blaming your emotions on someone else.

4. Request action

Can we … [insert proposal]?

E.g. *Can we agree that, if there is going to be an issue with meeting deadlines, we can speak candidly to each other about it well ahead of time?*

You are asking rather than demanding, so the other person can say no. If they do, you can discuss a different solution and, if necessary, go back to the beginning of the technique and begin again by expressing how you feel.

Note: In giraffe language, you don't make requests of the past, e.g., *It would have been nice if you had finished the work on time.*

Giraffe language responses don't condone or condemn the actions or words of others. Instead, by not judging, we communicate more powerfully our likes, dislikes and needs, in a non-combative way, which is much more effective in stimulating the change we are looking for.

Giraffe language in practice

Marshall Rosenberg was an American psychologist and peace mediator, and the creator of giraffe language.

When he was addressing a group of Palestinians in a refugee camp, a man stood up, pointed at Rosenberg and called him a murderer. Rosenberg concluded that the comments were associated with his American nationality; the night before, some tear gas canisters marked *Made in the USA* had been fired into the camp.

He responded with empathy. He asked the man, 'Are you angry because you would like my government to use its resources differently?' (Note here that Rosenberg's giraffe language puts you with you, in the same way it puts I with I.)

Rosenberg remembers that, as the dialogue continued, he listened for the feeling and need behind each statement. He didn't receive the man's words as attacks but felt grateful that this man was sharing his vulnerabilities with him. Gradually, the gentleman felt understood, and Rosenberg was able to explain his reason for being at the camp. An hour later, Rosenberg was at the gentleman's house, having been invited to join him for Ramadan dinner.

Rosenberg didn't reply with his own thoughts or justifications, and he didn't strive to meet this man's needs with practical solutions. He simply listened until it was clear the man felt he had been heard. Then he was able to communicate effectively.

Once we have learned to look for what the heart is saying behind any message, we discover we don't need to fear what someone else says. Their words are a reflection of their needs rather than a judgement on us.

OOPS, OUCH, WHOA

This tool offers a new language to employees who are reluctant to speak out when something sounds wrong. All of us have occasions when something unkind or unthoughtful is said, when we feel hurt or realise how someone else must feel, and it can be hard to know how to react. We might wonder if we're the only person with that opinion, we might not want to embarrass the other person, or we might simply not have the right language to challenge the other person on the spot.

Annaliese Griffin wrote an article, 'Three Words You Need for Your Next Hard Conversation', about a parenting workshop, where Shela Linton, an activist for social and racial inequality, taught her about *Oops, Ouch* and *Whoa.*

Here's how it works:

- If we say something that comes out wrong, which we suddenly realise is unkind or might cause offence, we say *Oops.*
- If someone else says something that makes us feel bad, we say *Ouch.* Whether or not the comments were directed at us, we can let the other person know that it may have had a different impact than they intended.
- If we're finding it hard to follow a conversation or a line of reasoning, or we aren't familiar with a concept or an acronym, we say *Whoa* and ask for clarification.

The speed and ease of these words helps to signal that mistakes are normal, they can be quickly remedied, and they don't have to be a big deal.

Ideally, these techniques are agreed and shared in company culture or at the beginning of a meeting. Even if they are not, someone expressing a relatively unprovocative response such as *Ouch* likely won't offend the perpetrator.

The immediacy of the response is crucial. It offers the opportunity to rectify unintentional language or behaviour, or to explain why clarification is needed. More important, it offers the chance for insight into and empathy for why a comment has caused someone pain. We can only *do* better when we *know* better. While I am a keen advocate for social justice, equality and equity, I know I'm not always up to date with the most woke terms. I need someone to say *Ouch* to me if I say the wrong thing. How else will I learn?

If holding ourselves to account can start with these three little words, which anyone can remember and put into action, perhaps we might all start to see more of the right behaviour.

THE LANGUAGE OF WORKPLACE LOVE – WHAT PEOPLE NEED TO HEAR

The book *The 5 Love Languages*, by Gary Chapman, outlines five ways that romantic partners express and experience their love:

1. Words of affirmation
2. Acts of service

3. Exchanging gifts
4. Quality time
5. Physical touch

The idea here is that the greater understanding we have of our own and our partner's experience of love, the stronger the relationship can be. We tend to express love the way we like to receive it, but it's more important to understand how our partners most like to experience love.

Translating this concept to the language of *workplace* love, we must first acknowledge that we have to put strict limitations on the option of physical touch. Please don't do anything that warrants the police being involved, but you can fist bump and high five away. All the other languages of love translate easily to the workplace, and we will create stronger bonds with our teams if we indulge their preferred language.

Remember: think about what is important to someone else. If they don't value receiving gifts (at work this might be simply a cup of coffee or doughnuts) but do value quality time, then this is how to prioritise your effort.

Think: do I know which language works best for my colleagues, team or manager?

GRATITUDE

Great communication includes expressions of gratitude. Thanking people for experiences, commitment, help, guidance or gifts has several ways of improving our happiness. We gain pleasure and self-esteem from helping to make other people happy. We retrain our thinking to more positive thoughts, which helps disrupt the hedonic treadmill so we start to appreciate the things we may have started to take for granted.

Christmas party

I can vividly remember attending my first work Christmas conference in 2001. It was a whole day and night event in a lovely hotel in the centre of London, with about 300 attendees. I was blown away by everything that had been laid on for us. From video presentations by the board through to an awards ceremony in the evening, accompanied by pyrotechnic displays and fantastic catering – I had never attended anything so big and impressive.

The next day, I thought about who I could contact to thank for the experience, but in the end I didn't. I didn't have the managing director's email address, and anyway, I decided it would make me look like a kiss ass. It just didn't feel like the sort of thing people did, and anyway, the managing director would already know the event had been successful, right?

Looking back, now that I have arranged events and experiences for employees, I recognise how super-proud, appreciated and amazing I feel when a few employees get in touch to say thanks. I'm also sure those people have felt great when they've had my response, knowing that a small gesture made a big difference to my happiness. All in all, a few minutes writing a thank-you note creates a heart-warming, reciprocal effect.

We thank people all the time in our lives – at the supermarket checkout, when the babysitter is leaving, getting off the bus. Why does gratitude feel less natural in the workplace?

While simple gestures of smiles and thanks, high fives and pats on the back are wonderful, the impact of increased effort in giving gratitude is significant. Taking someone aside to specifically thank them, writing a note they can look back on in years to come or buying a thoughtful gift has the effect of improving baseline happiness for both parties.

PHRASES TO USE OR STRICTLY AVOID AT WORK

Even if we are in control of how we feel and respond to people's actions and words, many of our habitual phrases may have a patronising or insensitive implied meaning for some. It's nearly always easy, though, to ask or say the same thing without any potential misunderstanding. If we are careful to avoid any hint of sarcasm, criticism or insensitivity, we are guaranteed to get better responses from others, build better relationships and help make the workplace an altogether happier environment.

Here are some simple examples, which will help you to consider how best to word any other phrases you use.

Phrases to say	**Tacit meaning**	**Impact**
I was thinking about our last conversation	I'm interested in you	Recipient feels valued
I took your advice	I'm open to learning; thanks for helping	Recipient feels empowered
I love your energy	I'm grateful for positivity	Recipient feels appreciated and will keep the energy going

Phrases not to say	**Tacit meaning**	**Impact**	**Alternative**
As I said before As mentioned in my previous email	Did you not listen/read properly the first time? Dumbass	Recipient feels stupid and/or annoyed at your indignance	Simply repeat what they need to know without pointing out you have said it already
Good luck with that	You won't succeed	Sarcasm isn't appealing	I hope you're successful (said unsarcastically)

Phrases not to say	**Tacit meaning**	**Impact**	**Alternative**
I'm really busy	I'm important because I'm so busy	Recipient feels you don't see the value in making time for them	Can I help you in a second / at lunchtime?
With all due respect …	It's never with all due respect. This is simply a habitual phrase, as insensitive as *No offence, but …*	Recipient thinks they're about to be given a rollocking	Simply say what you were going to say without this snarky phrase ever entering your lexicon
I don't care It makes no difference to me	I'm not interested	Recipient feels they and/or their work isn't valued	Both are great – you choose
You should have …	I know best	Recipient feels blame	I recommend ...

Much like the gym, but much less sweatily, the more we practise being deliberate with our language, and following a formula for communicating well, the easier and more habitual it becomes. It has a wonderful snowball effect too – people receiving language in a certain way are more likely to start being kinder and more sensitive when talking to others.

Most of us have a deep yearning to help other people, and kind words are an excellent way to fulfil that need. Before we know it, a culture once permeated with a little too much ego can be reformed to one where people are energised by offering kind words. Seeing colleagues puff out their chests with self-esteem is far more cathartic than the reaction we'll get from venting, judging, blaming and backbiting. Workplace communication isn't ever going to be flawless, but if there are enough displays of intentional positivity and kindness, the occasions of reactive behaviour and punitive language will become outliers.

As the great philosopher Hafiz said, 'The words you speak become the house you live in.' We can create happier workplaces by being impeccable with our words. And we all want to live in nice houses.

CHAPTER SUMMARY

This chapter has illuminated the fact that communication is much more complex than we might first acknowledge. The number of variables at play and the tiny subtle nuances that make or break communication mean that it's an area for dedicated study and practice. It is not as simple as maintaining eye contact or having a firm handshake, as some workshops might spend too long impressing on you. The beauty of great communication lies in the blend of communication with emotional intelligence.

The way we communicate is hugely impacted by our needs, thoughts and emotions, and those of others. What we say and do depends on what's going on for us and how much attention we pay to our interactions. If we improve our awareness of what we're thinking and feeling and we can control our instinctual responses, we have half of the formula for creating better interactions. When we piece this together with the same consideration of our colleagues' needs, thoughts and emotions, we will conduct more thoughtful, selfless, careful interactions, which undoubtedly lead to happier employment.

KEY REMINDERS FROM THIS CHAPTER

- Remember the ladder of inference. Everything we see, read or hear is processed by our unique brains, so we naturally make judgements, assumptions, shortcuts, and interpretations that are based on our thoughts, values and experiences in life. What we interpret is not necessarily the truth, so let's give each other a break and shift our starting point to assuming positive intent.

- We don't want to damage people's self-esteem, but we do want to help others see what we see. Offer feedback on people's behaviour, not on their character.

- Feedback is one of the biggest hurdles for company culture and happier workplaces. COIN and giraffe language allow us to have assertive and caring conversations. We can also all practise receiving feedback and work on diminishing the feelings of defensiveness, justification and blame that can arise when we simply feel a bit hurt.

- *Oops, Ouch, Whoa* is a must for any business, to make sure errors are dealt with in the moment and without judgement. Saying the wrong thing is human. Dealing with it behind closed doors or not at all is toxic for any culture.
- Think about how you interact in the workplace. Do you give people love in the way that they like to receive it or in the way you like to give it? If you don't know how they prefer to be loved, ask!

CHAPTER 9

RETHINKING MANAGEMENT

One of the reasons for the success of the TV series *The Office* is because it portrays a boss and an environment that are instantly relatable for viewers. From the comfort and protection of their own homes, people relive some of their own unfortunate experiences as they watched cringeworthy interactions play out on screen. These are headed up by the show's co-writer, Ricky Gervais, who plays the leading role of the clueless and arrogant middle manager, David Brent.

Bad management is ubiquitous in organisations, but here's the thing: it's not necessarily the fault of the managers. As we learned in Chapter 7, traditional hierarchies primarily dictate that the only way to progress is by moving into management. A combination of an employee's desire for growth and their desire to earn more and to increase their status means that most have a crack at management, and organisations support most employees in this. However, the manager role requires such an array of skills, many of which are rarely fully assessed or taught. It should therefore probably be no surprise that some guise of David Brent might be stewarding our careers at some point. There are of course many wonderful managers out there, although they are in the minority, as we will shortly cover.

The heady expectation from a business owner or leader – that any manager should match their own levels of competence – is also a burdensome load to carry, especially when coupled with the eager eyes of an employee who (at least at the start) believes their manager is some sort of celestial being with the wisdom of Yoda.

The role of manager is unforgiving at times and delightfully rewarding at others. In this chapter we will first explore how we might rethink management within the pyramid hierarchy of a traditional organisation. We will then delve into the more radical world of managerless organisations, whose structure, culture, and operations reject almost all conventional business practices.

Whether we opt for tweaks or radical change, the current ideology of management must evolve. Statistically, anecdotally and televisually, it is contributing significantly to employees' disengagement in the workplace.

HOW DO WE DO MANAGEMENT NOW?

The difference between a great manager and a poor one is palpable. According to *Harvard Business Review*, less than 50% of employees have a high degree of trust in their peers and managers. *Ouch.* Productivity, absenteeism, engagement, happiness and customer satisfaction are all impacted by the quality of a manager. It would therefore be reasonable to expect that the process for selecting managers would be complex, filled with tests, case studies, behavioural assessments and reviews from peers.

In reality, though, how do we go about selecting these paragons of engagement? Generally, selection is based on three main factors:

1. Tenure – an employee who has been with a business for some time needs somewhere to progress to (often out of fear of them progressing to another company)
2. Competence in the pre-managerial job
3. Leadership deciding ad hoc who has the qualities to be promoted – rarely are team members invited to comment on who they feel would be best placed to manage them

The tricky thing is that none of these criteria is effective in determining who will be a great manager. Knowledge of subject matter is important: part of a manager's job is to drive outcomes and productivity, which is easier if they have achieved a good level of proficiency in the subject. But what about all the other qualities that are vital in a managerial role, such as empathy, trust and communication? While we find reference to these skills and qualities in job specifications and adverts, I'm not convinced they are sufficiently assessed.

THE MANAGER

In 2008 Google set out to determine what makes a great manager and launched an internal research team for Project Oxygen. Their findings, which highlighted eight key competencies, sculpted their management training and their management surveys. By publicising and training their managers on these most important types of behaviour, they saw improvement in turnover, satisfaction and performance. After further surveys, Google expanded on their original eight behaviours, adding the capabilities numbered 9 and 10 below.

The ten behaviours of Google's best managers:

1. Is a good coach
2. Empowers team and does not micromanage
3. Creates an inclusive team environment, showing concern for success and wellbeing
4. Is productive and results-orientated
5. Is a good communicator – listens and shares information
6. Supports career development and discusses performance
7. Has a clear vision/strategy for the team
8. Has key technical skills to help advise the team
9. Collaborates across Google
10. Is a strong decision maker

You may note quickly that this list is heavily biased towards softer skills.

If you thought about yourself, your own manager or a manager that reports to you, how would you rate their performance against these ten criteria?

According to Gallup, only about one in ten employees possesses *high* talent to manage. The good news is that a further two in ten possess *basic* management talent, which can be developed to a high level with investment in training and development, taking us to three out of ten in total. However, if organisations typically promote on tenure, technical ability and gut instinct, they stand a seven in ten chance of getting management completely wrong.

An author and expert in engagement and management, Marcus Buckingham, draws the analogy between managing people and chess to explain how great managers work. Great managers note that all of their pieces move differently, in different directions and with different capabilities. Average managers play checkers rather than chess so move each uniform piece in the same way as another.

Only by understanding the characteristics and strengths of employees and by learning how to coordinate skills in a team can the manager help ascend a team to its full potential.

Imagine if the alteration we had to make in selecting managers was highlighting the employees who knew the most about their team or who were the best at understanding others' motivations. Rather than promotion to manager being about individual previous performance and experience, it could include metrics around relationships, emotional intelligence, and motivation.

Leaders are generally reticent to promote employees based on their ideal management skills, i.e., the softer-skills elements identified by Google. Many leaders believe a team can't respect a manager who is a less successful technical performer than others within the team.

Fergusson vs Maradona

Alec Fergusson had a successful footballing career, playing notably for Rangers and Scotland in the 1960s. He was, by all accounts, a great footballer.

Was Fergusson as good a footballer as those he later came to manage – Ronaldo, Beckham, Scholes, Giggs, Cantona? Likely not. But did those players doubt his ability as a manager because they regarded themselves as better footballers? Not for a second.

Conversely, Maradona is regarded as one of the greatest footballers of all time, yet he made a shocking job of management. He was appointed manager of Argentina in 2008, to much fanfare, and scraped Argentina through to qualify for the 2010 World Cup. After a successful group stage, Argentina lumbered past Mexico before being destroyed by Germany in the quarter finals, and Maradona's underwhelming tactical play was held to account. He subsequently had a disastrous stint at UAE club Al-Wasl, after which he hung up his managerial boots.

If we are to consistently increase the quality of management within our businesses, we must shift our mindset to seek out the three out of ten people who have high or basic genuine management talent.

It's not only leaders and organisations (and football clubs) that need the mindset shift. Employees need to view management differently too.

DRAW A DIFFERENT PICTURE

A sprinter will spend most of their early life learning and practising how to be the best sprinter they can be. Usain Bolt set the world record in 2009, running the 100-metre sprint in 9.58 seconds. A decathlete will dedicate themselves to reaching their potential across ten different events, one of which is the 100 metres. Olympic 2020 decathlete champion Damian Warner ran the 100 m in the decathlon in only 10.12 seconds, i.e., not far off the leading athlete in that single event.

How do we compare the excellence of these two athletes? Do we view either as more or less talented or capable than the other? I think most people find Bolt running that fast equally as impressive as Damian excelling in ten different events.

What if we could view professional excellence in the business context with the same lens? What if organisations had cultures that valued the status of those who excelled in one particular field as much as they valued those who excelled across a number of fields? Both types of people illustrate potential being stretched in different directions. The technical expert (the sprinter) becomes super-fast in one particular skill – what I see as a vertical line. Meanwhile, the multi-eventer (the decathlete) reaches their potential through the horizontal breadth of their skills, even if they are less capable than an expert in any one particular field.

In his *Harvard Business Review* article 'Managing Without Managers', Semco CEO Richard Semler explains that, in his business, the applications engineer who can identify from drawings that one particular pump on a ship will fail in arctic temperatures is hugely more valuable to the business. He is therefore paid significantly more than the person who manages his unit.

If we change the status and reward attached to positions, employees can start to consider the duties of every role with more objectivity, clarity and interest. Assessing their strengths and choosing the best role for their growth is not only better for business – it's also better for everyone's happiness.

Businesses reap the benefits of their employees' natural strengths and desire for growth if responsibilities are undertaken by those with the greatest aptitude for them.

The question would no longer be: Who is the best employee to be manager?

It would be: *How do we drive a whole team's potential by orientating to strengths?*

Organisations could offer the opportunity for their people to be leaders and managers, but leaders of a behaviour, purpose or skill rather than only of people. Consequently, we might find that this wider, lateral pyramid structure creates an atmosphere of peership and more parity of importance.

We could see the creation of roles such as team visionary, purpose leader, training leviathan, customer experience promoter, labour economist and disruption instigator. All these roles could move the individual and business further towards their potential and improve the value offered … and none of them need the title of manager.

An English training company, Happy, introduced the practice that employees have two managers. One is responsible for elements such as monitoring tasks, decision making and direction setting. The other is responsible for interpersonal aspects such as coaching, challenging and supporting. Interestingly, the leadership appoint the manager responsible for decision making and reporting, and the team choose the manager for the interpersonal skills. (You can read *The Happy Manifesto* by Henry Stewart for more information.)

Messier organograms? Yes.

But roles better suited to people and greater engagement? Definitely.

Complexity of reporting lines should not inhibit businesses from drawing a different picture.

OLD SCHOOL AND NEW SCHOOL

The modern era of work is awash with calls for managers to demonstrate empathy, care and concern for wellbeing, and rightly so. These characteristics have often been lacking in management of the past. I have noticed that many managers and leaders, especially those whose careers have spanned over 20 years so far, are concerned that empathy, care and nurturing could breed a workforce of flaky individuals who lack resilience.

Those leaders don't raise this concern openly, as they either aspire to grow with modern management techniques and/or realise how taboo it could sound. If the current workplace ideology could be described as empathetic and nurturing, the ideology of 20 years ago might be summarised as some version of *Shut up and get on with it*. This isn't to say that nurturing and stewardship didn't take place at all. However, it was generally felt that resilience increased if we quit bleating and sorted things out for ourselves. Of course, this approach had its own issues, and it bred a workplace generation that struggled to communicate feelings with each other and were probably unhappier and less collaborative because of that.

The best coaches appear to be those who employ a mixture of push and pull.

The push approach is ideal when you feel you have pushed yourself to your very limit and every part of you wants to stop. Your coach will compel you to do more – a version of *Shut up and get on with it*. Their words don't have to be excessively hard; they should be encouraging and unequivocal. If you have taken a personal training session, for example, these are the coaches who keep persuading you to do one more lap or one more rep. They find a little more in you and keep pushing you to achieve more.

The pull approach is about when you have pushed yourself to your limit and every part of you wants to stop, but your coach takes you to one side, listens, understands, and reminds you what is possible and why you are working so hard for it. The choice to carry on is yours, but they may even jog alongside you to help you eke out another lap.

Most important is to strike the engagement balance with teams at work. We can't use so much push that we drive people to disengage from the manager or the task. We must use enough to enable people to push through challenges and to reach a new level. And we can't use so much pull that people settle for comfort or their growth is slow. Rather, we need enough to foster engagement over a longer period.

The skill of a manager or coach is to know how much push and pull each team member needs and when to proffer which. This dovetails with Marcus Buckingham's reference to great managers playing chess rather than draughts. One thing is for sure: managers need empathy to select the right approach and to see when they have picked the wrong one. The new school are onto something, for sure.

Too much push

In 2006 I walked into the office of my then employer to find a can of highly caffeinated energy drink on my desk, with Prodigy's 'I'm a Firestarter' being blasted at nightclub-volume level from an enormous amp in the corner of the office. It transpired that this was a new motivational technique dreamt up by my manager.

The idea was that we would vigorously start making sales calls at 8 am, as quickly and effectively as we could. After each call, we were to drink a shot of the energy drink. Any reluctance to make the calls or guzzle the shots was met with considerable disdain from our manager.

After about 45 minutes of this authoritarian, despotic, forced culture change, one colleague, Dave, stood up from his desk, uttered something about having had enough of this crap and slammed his phone down. Maddened by his defiance and disobedience, our manager shouted to him from the other side of the office. Dave ignored him for a few seconds, holding his head in his hands and pacing the three steps around his desk. Our manager became increasingly irate, his voice growing louder and more insistent. The rest of us ended our sales calls, desperate to witness what would unfold. When the manager went over and put his hand on Dave's shoulder, Dave exploded and aggressively slapped the manager's hand away, with a barrage of expletives. Without pause, he then turned around to his desk, picked up his landline phone, ripped it out of its socket and proceeded to throw it across a bank of desks.

We all sat in stunned silence as we waited for the next move. Dave began collecting his things as our manager shouted at him to get out of the office, but it seems Dave realised he could revel in one final act of defiance. He sat back down in his chair and pulled himself into his desk, refusing to leave.

Our manager ended up calling the police, explaining that an employee wouldn't leave the office after being fired. Dave looked delighted with the disruption he was causing and, when the time came, listened briefly to the police officer, before yelling further profanities and departing.

The legend of Dave's disobedience became infamous, and it helped to restore our (dignity and) confidence in making our manager aware that we weren't enjoying his interpretation of a results-orientated, work-hard-play-hard culture.

MANAGER ENGAGEMENT

In 'Only 35% of U.S. Managers Are Engaged in Their Jobs', Gallup uses a term called the *cascade effect* to describe where an employee's engagement is directly influenced by their manager's engagement … whose engagement is directly influenced by their manager's engagement. Disengagement, like many other attitudes, can be contagious.

Employees should recognise that motivation isn't only a downward movement. It's within everyone's control to motivate upwards, downwards, and side to side.

Managers, who already carry a significant load, often find their own engagement is sidelined or deprioritised in favour of that of their team members. A 2016 report by Forbes highlighted research illustrating that 98% of managers felt they needed more training to deal with key challenges such as professional development, employee retention, time management and conflict resolution. Organisations must remember that investing in their managers' needs and motivation is as essential as investing in those of the team. The impact of doing so – or failing to do so – is far wider reaching than managers' personal development.

MEASURE YOUR MANAGER

You've possibly heard the phrase *You can't manage what you can't measure.* It's a popular, sensible idiom, which tends to be applied to the manager, based on the team's results. While this is vital, there are other measurements around attrition, absenteeism and engagement that provide a rounder picture.

Sure, companies have engagement surveys, which ask for general information about managers and leadership. But what if we took this further? In order for managers to create happy teams, why don't we measure managers' accountability against the metrics the team or business feel are most important?

For example, Google asks employees to assess the performance of their manager via a Likert scale survey, based on the ten behaviours identified from their research listed earlier in this chapter.

The employee reads a number of statements and then rates their managers on a scale of 1 (strongly disagree) to 5 (strongly agree). The statements include whether the employee would recommend their manager to others, how the manager communicates, whether they provide development opportunities, how effectively they make tough decisions, etc. The employee is invited to provide free commentary next to any of their ratings, and to comment on behaviours they would like their manager to continue or to change. The results provide the basis for great development conversations with the manager, and a data capture that can be measured against in 3/6/12 months' time.

This is a great tool for checking in on managers' self-awareness and self-acceptance, and on their desire to grow. It's an opportunity for the managers to exhibit vulnerability, and it is made richer if the manager can listen with openness and curiosity to what was behind their team's ratings and comments.

Perhaps a better idiom could be *You can't manage unless you're ready to measure yourself.*

To ensure that identified areas of development are not forgotten, the team and manager must agree an accountability process for the period between surveys. For example, if consideration for the employee is an aspect chosen for development, they could set objectives around allowing plenty of time to talk, asking about employees' friends and family, sharing experiences, asking questions that dig deeper than work, or making one gesture a week that shows each of the team the manager is thinking of them as an individual.

This may seem contrived at first, but as employees recognise and embrace their managers' efforts, everyone will start to appreciate the improvements, and this whole process will become normal.

Not only can managers use these survey results as a stimulus for their own learning and growth, but companies can also use them as the basis for performance reviews of their managers. We may wish to alter the above to those behaviours that are important in our organisation's manager roles, and adapt the questions accordingly. Only if organisations hold managers to account for focus on the softer skills of the role, as well as the hard results, will we see managers' performance tangibly improve.

HOW TO MANAGE ME

Imagine if your manager gave you a handbook on day one in your new job. Not the staff handbook or a training manual – a handbook called *How to manage me* – on how to manage your new manager.

As described in *The Wall Street Journal* article 'Job Candidates Get a Manual From Boss: "How to Handle Me"', in 2003 Ron B Goodspeed, president and CEO of a large hospitals group in Massachusetts, created such a handbook as part of his process to identify a new member of his board. This had been recommended by psychologist Laurence J Stybel, who had wondered why, if even the most basic electronic devices come with operating manuals, managers shouldn't also come with instructions.

Goodspeed drafted a copy and circulated it around his executive team, who suggested revisions and additions. He said that, in reviewing his own development, the handbook 'keeps you on track – as opposed to learning a year later that you got off track'.

The process of developing the manual not only generated useful insight for Goodspeed but also created confidence within the team in speaking more directly and openly. Creating this platform for honest feedback and continual improvement served many purposes, not least for the new vice president, Patrick Gannon, who received the manual two days before he started in his new job. Gannon read the document several times and commented, 'This is really very helpful because it saves a lot of time figuring out what the boss thinks of things. My respect for him went up a notch.'

A draft *How to manage me* manual might look like this, with three clear chapters:

DO (what I want to see more of) …

1. Come to me with the problem and the solution
2. Be positive and optimistic, with a dose of reality
3. Give accurate worst-case and best-case revenue forecasting
4. Be yourself and talk to me about you and your life outside of work
5. Lead by example and be the best version of yourself
6. Constantly learn and bring new thoughts to the table
7. Take responsibility for your own career and development
8. Remember the bigger picture and what we are trying to achieve

PERMISSION (you might think I don't want this, but I really do) …

1. To make mistakes
2. To change your mind
3. To be upset
4. To challenge me when I seem too set on something without good reason
5. To tell me if you are struggling
6. To be vulnerable
7. To stop me from being too verbose

DON'T (do not do these things!) …

1. Interrupt me in the middle of something, unless it's urgent
2. Behave defensively or justify behaviour
3. Speak ill of anyone or be unkind with your words, even when they're not listening
4. Be concerned only with the things that are your responsibility

Every how-to-manage-me document would not only aid self-awareness; it would also serve as part of a personal development plan. This could be rolled out to employees too – after all, if we can find any ways of helping to understand ourselves and others better, shouldn't we all do it? Personally, I can't believe that we don't already all come with instructions.

HIRE NO MANAGERS – TEAL ORGANISATIONS

Wait. What?

Particularly since the publication of Frederic Laloux's incredible book, *Reinventing Organizations*, there has been a growing fascination with a new style of business structure. Dissatisfied with the 100-year-old management model designed for factories, and of the idea that employees are sheep that need shepherding, more and more businesses are warming up to a revolution in management. In fact, this isn't even about management – it's about being management-less.

While the focus on organisation structure received a new boost from Laloux in 2014, organisations operating with radically different structures and cultures have been around for over 40 years.

We shouldn't be surprised. Businesses that have become overladen with management are described as fat and bloated, and management is seen by some as the biggest factor in making people *unproductive*. Some therefore believe that the idea of managers enhancing the work of their team is a misnomer. But how far do employees and organisations want to go? How radically do organisations need to be disrupted?

Laloux coined the term *Teal organisation* in his 2014 book. The Teal movement describes an ideology that has principles but no specific guidelines and which advocates, amongst other things, self-management by employees.

Laloux classified organisations by colour, reflecting the era and ideology behind each organisation's systems and culture. Most 21st-century businesses currently operate in the orange zone, while some such as TOMS or Patagonia have evolved to green, as outlined in the table below.

	Features	**Ideology**
Orange	• Innovation • Accountability • Meritocracy	The goal is to beat competition, achieve profit and growth and manage by objectives (command and control on the what; freedom on the how).
Green	• Empowerment • Values-driven • Stakeholder model	Within the classic pyramid structure, focus is on culture and empowerment to achieve extraordinary employee motivation.

	Features	Ideology
Teal	• Self-management	Self-management is organised via small teams who take responsibility for their own governance.
	• Wholeness	Wholeness is shown in the belief that each colleague (employee) is of fundamental equal worth and at work we can be the truest expression of ourselves.
	• Purpose	Evolutionary purpose is viewing the organisation as an organism that has a soul and purpose of its own.

At first glance, the Teal concept may seem a bit wacky or spiritual for our everyday workplace. Many of us have never known or tried anything like this, and we tend to like what we're used to.

> **Teal allows *anyone* in the organisation to make *any* decision, provided they follow the Teal process.**

The Teal process predominantly revolves around seeking advice. Anyone wanting to make a decision first needs to talk to people who know more about the issue, and to anyone who will be affected by the decision. Even if those groups disagree with the proposal, it might still go ahead, but the advice process needs to be followed.

The idea of employee accountability – expedient decision making, meaningful work, profit participation, fewer meetings, and playing to employees' strengths – sounds wonderfully happy. But seriously, can it actually work?

Perhaps surprisingly, there are over 200 Teal businesses that have been operating in this maverick, employee-led way – some for 30–40 years – and these businesses are employers of hundreds and sometimes thousands of people. Their pioneering ways can help us understand how it is possible to democratise and organise a system for huge teams of people, while creating growth for the business and far happier employment than most pyramid organisations.

In *Reinventing Organizations,* Laloux offers great insight into FAVI, a family-owned, French brass foundry business. FAVI operated as a traditional pyramid organisation until new CEO Jean-Francois Zobrist was appointed in 1983. Within two years, Zobrist had transformed the business into self-managed teams of 15 to 50 employees, predominantly dedicated to a specific customer.

The company has no middle management and no processes, other than those created within its own teams. Traditional departments such as HR, planning, scheduling and production no longer exist.

FAVI is the only manufacturer of its kind left in Europe. It boasts high profit margins, salaries well above average, and the exemplary record of not delivering a single order late in over 25 years. Staff turnover is virtually non-existent, and most employees cannot fathom returning to a traditional pyramid organisation.

Because decisions are made within the team, they can be made with speed and specific knowledge. Meetings are predominantly ad hoc, called only when an opportunity arises or a topic requires discussion. This helps to eradicate meeting paralysis and ensures that those impacted by decisions are present to contribute, rather than decisions being made at high levels without specific expertise or hands-on experience.

In Teal organisations all decisions are made within the team, but a team of regional coaches exists to offer advice and share experiences. These coaches are selected specifically for their coaching ability and are there to ask insightful questions, mirror unhelpful behaviour to teams or – if absolutely necessary – suggest that a team pauses to deal with a serious issue. The regional coaches have no decision-making power, no budget and no targets. They exist purely for the wellbeing and smooth development of teams as self-managed organisms.

The final element I have selected from Laloux's examination of FAVI's operational systems and culture is that of trust. Shortly after taking over as CEO, Zobrist decided spontaneously to get rid of the production targets in the factory because he trusted the team to work as efficiently and productively as they could. His management team were aghast and Zobrist was worried – so much so that he checked the numbers every day for a week. When he found at the end of the week that the productivity numbers had actually increased, he was curious. The workers explained that they had deliberately slowed down their work in case the targets might otherwise subsequently be increased by management. They also shared that they naturally worked to a physiological rhythm, and they had been deliberately working more slowly. Once the productivity targets were removed, they simply returned to their natural rhythm.

Trust breeds accountability (just as accountability breeds trust) and offers employees the opportunity to be treated as adults inside the workplace, just as they are outside of work. Employees in Teal organisations are trusted to set their own remuneration through a process of role evaluation, ranking systems and peer advice, based on a calibration of remuneration across colleagues. Employees can choose whether or not to accept peer advice, and their salary is then made public.

> **Teal organisations find that trust and peer pressure regulate behaviour better than the command and control of hierarchical management.**

Another stalwart of self-management is multimillion-dollar Brazilian business Semco Partners, which has multifaceted business endeavours covering industrial manufacturing, property, technology and service sectors, amongst others. When Ricardo Semler, aged 21, took over the business from his father in 1980, he immediately fired 60% of managers in his quest to create a decentralised business. The business grew from US $4 million in 1982 to $212 million in 2003. The business's innovation and diversification accounted for the majority of growth – innovation that was put forward by the employees.

Ricardo Semler discusses Semco's path out of authoritarian command and control into a democratised culture in his *Harvard Business Review* article 'Managing Without Managers'. The article is well worth a read in its entirety, but some notable features of their operation are:

- They don't hire or promote people until they have been interviewed and accepted by all their future team members.
- Twice a year, the team members evaluate their managers; and twice a year, everyone in the company completes an anonymous questionnaire about company credibility and manager competence.
- Semco treat their teams like adults and believe in emergent leadership – whoever is best placed to lead the team will naturally evolve into that role. There is structure to their organisation, but the structure is not imposed from above. People can fall somewhat naturally into their own roles. Roles are deemed equally important (although not of equal skill, experience,

etc), and leaders will emerge voluntarily, albeit not in title.

At the time of writing, Semco has outperformed its competitors and the economy for over 40 years with the use of:

- Collegial decision making
- Teams of 150 employees
- Throwing out the rule book
- Rotating jobs every two to five years
- Eliminating time clocks
- Offering complete financial transparency

Functioning in this way takes time to establish, but the results are evident. One can correlate Semco's financial success with their impressive 1–2% employee turnover.

The success of a Teal organisation depends as much on the employees' desire for and success in collective responsibility and egalitarian decision making, as it does on the owner's ability to relinquish control. For example, Ricardo Semler found himself outvoted by his employees when he sought to acquire another business. This exemplifies how Teal has to work – it has to be all in. There aren't reserved rights; there aren't special circumstances when the egalitarian culture doesn't apply; and the owner and CEO don't get to make their own independent decisions.

WHO CAN MAKE TEAL WORK?

FAVI and Semco are just two examples of the many large organisations that have adopted Teal culture, practices and beliefs. Others include:

- Morning Star, a $700 million tomato-processing business
- WL Gore, famous for its trademark product, GORE-TEX
- Valve, an American gaming company
- Alcoholics Anonymous

All these operate with managerless systems, demonstrating how the model can work in any sector, industry and business size as well as in non-profit organisations.

The major force behind making Teal organisations work is the people. Leaders are different, hiring is different, and the culture is different. Because Teal organisations are still very much in the minority, hiring for Teal poses a new set of challenges. We see from the example above that leaders must fully embrace the ideology that everyone is of equal power and everyone has the opportunity to make a decision. Ricardo Semler was outvoted by Semco's employees on a major business acquisition he proposed – the employees felt it was the wrong time and Semler accepted their decision. A Teal business leader needs to be prepared for such eventualities and must accept that the process and practices must be honoured at all times and by everyone, or it will make a mockery of the entire concept and values.

The Teal process is not inflexible. Many great solutions have been found for complex problems by coordinating the voices of large teams of people on company intranets or simply on the factory floor. The fact that employees vote for and create the solutions means that the consequences of those decisions are more palatable than if the decisions have been imposed.

Most of the Teal organisations studied by Laloux made a transition to Teal from an orange-zone organisation, and it took a couple of years before practices and culture were truly engrained.

Careful attention is paid in the hiring process to explain the nature of Teal organisations, and to identify whether applicants have the right attitude and behaviour to work in a self-managed business. Teal isn't for everyone, and the companies appreciate that it can take some time to get used to. However, given that uncommonly low attrition rates and high employee engagement are common threads of Teal organisations, it's clear that employees being able to coordinate and make their own choices, to understand more about the business than they might ever do in a top-down pyramid, and to be treated as adults, creates a successful organisational culture. Perhaps even the epitome.

AN EQUILIBRIUM OF STATUS

The choice of organisational structure and division of responsibility lie with business leaders, and one can see why they might be inclined to perpetuate the pyramid hierarchy – not only because they're used to it, but because the pyramid accentuates leaders' and managers' status and esteem. A Teal organisation's equilibrium of power and authority isn't appealing to all leaders.

By rethinking management, we embrace all employees' desire for growth and autonomy, not only that of the leaders and managers, thereby maximising the full potential of the workforce.

SYSTEMS

When I began learning about Teal organisations, one aspect particularly confused me. I understood that employees made decisions in teams about anything from salary levels to budgets for equipment, but it initially sounded like a crazy free-for-all. I couldn't believe that everyone in teams could amiably decide the fate of other team members, or that everyone would adopt the greater-good ideology to make selfless decisions. The possibility that everyone would reach benign compromises on decisions also didn't feel like a preferable alternative to traditional pyramid organisations. When we compromise, it tends to mean at least one party will be disappointed with the outcome, if not all involved.

In fact, I had all of these things wrong.

> **Teal organisations are not system-less. They have created a *different* set of principles and practices for how they operate.**

Let's think of an example of a basic decision within any company: a budget for a new piece of equipment. In a traditional pyramid organisation, if an employee recognised the need for the new equipment, they would most likely ask their manager, who would present it up the chain of command until it reached the appropriate level of decision maker. That person would make their decision based on budgetary constraints (that only they are privy to), on the information that has been passed up the line, and probably on their own independent judgement of the benefit of the new equipment.

In a Teal organisation, an employee would decide that the new piece of equipment would add value to their business and customers. They would find out the cost information and practicalities and would seek advice from all affected parties and people with expertise in the matter, including on budget. The employee would be under no obligation to accept the advice that came back; they would make decisions based on the widest information available and taking the opinions of their peers into account.

Decisions are not made by consensus. They are made with information, humility, trust and ownership. This doesn't stifle innovation – it equips decision makers to understand a broad spectrum of experience, make an informed decision and be accountable for it. Interestingly, the budget and complexity of an idea would determine how many people should offer advice, but as most Teal organisations offer complete financial transparency, employees are better equipped to present a case of cost versus potential reward.

WHAT DOESN'T WORK IN TEAL

For all the businesses that have made Teal a success, there are probably as many that have tried and failed. Social media company Medium announced in 2016 that they had decided to move back from a model similar to Teal, which they had implemented. They reported that they found it difficult to coordinate efforts at scale because of the need to coordinate across functions and gain alignment.

In his article 'What We Got Wrong When We Tried Flat Management', the co-founder of software application business Buffer, Leo Widrich, highlighted other failings. These included that people were easily lost – the amount of freedom they had with no guidance or accountability was overwhelming.

Self-management means that everyone is accountable for sorting out problems such as that of underperforming colleagues, which in a pyramid organisation would ordinarily fall on the shoulders of the manager. A manager being responsible for dealing with dilemmas saves the sanctity of team dynamics and personal relationships, which would be more difficult to protect with the whole team's involvement in decision making.

Many of the ideals within Teal feel in line with the evolving needs of modern-day businesses. If attitudes to work are changing, the structure of organisations must follow suit. Employees want, in the most part, to participate and for their opinions to be valued.

Those who can sign up to Teal and make it work clearly reap the rewards. Those who don't make it work might simply confuse their employees with a half-baked – if well-meant – attempt. Employees will quickly tire of the next big idea, so organisations must not take the trendy, attractive idea of being managerless lightly, thinking of it as the antidote for what doesn't currently work for them in their managerful organisation. Employers also need to accept that not everyone wants the mental burden of decision making – some are happier being followers rather than leaders.

The desire to disrupt traditional organisational structure is gathering momentum, and we can benefit from observing those who have tried – successfully or unsuccessfully – to develop or disrupt traditional practices. As more and more people get to know that Teal organisations exist, at least there can be better-informed moves towards joining or creating them. At the very least, all of us can cherry-pick great ideas from Teal innovations and practices. For example, Semco's practices of subordinates evaluating managers twice a year, and of interviewees for future roles being vetted and selected by the team into which they will be recruited, sound eminently sensible to me. Even in pyramid organisations, these ideas could help improve selection and hiring processes.

Encouraging great ideas or innovation from anywhere in the organisation is a fantastic part of Teal. In traditional organisations either this opportunity is not offered readily, or employees say they want to participate but rarely step up. Teal organisations undoubtedly generate innovation better than via the suggestions box in a traditional organisation.

The evidence shows that getting management right – whether that's in redesigning hiring practices, rethinking the manager role, or creating a different organisational structure for shared responsibility – can make a significant difference to the performance of an organisation.

CHAPTER SUMMARY

With expectations coming from both directions, and the need to please both parties, the manager's role is guaranteed to be challenging.

Appointment, recruitment, training and development for managers would benefit from an overhaul. In this chapter we have explored options for minor variations in the role, through to throwing the baby out with the bath water.

If we are to engage our teams and colleagues, we must engage our managers and rethink their roles. A manager's happiness and that of their teams depend on getting this role right.

KEY REMINDERS FROM THIS CHAPTER

- Consider which elements of a manager's role can be distributed to others. Could allocating certain responsibilities to team members offer them opportunity for growth?
- Think about whether and how much your team really needs to be managed. What specifically do they need?
- Promotion to manager would benefit from clear criteria around softer skills as well as technical prowess. If companies can define the behaviours and competencies a manager must possess in their business, these can be better tested during the recruitment or internal promotion process.
- Think about the push/pull narrative for coaching. Do you and your team use more push than pull, or vice versa?
- Teal organisations use an advice process for decision making, whereby any member of the team can bring an idea to the table, seek advice from experts and then decide whether to go ahead. Could you move elements of a traditional business structure to create more autonomy and innovation in key areas?

CHAPTER 10

MAXIMISE YOUR WORKFORCE

Teams provide the physical and emotional energy that propels individuals to greater heights. In *Big Potential* Shawn Achor coined a great phrase: 'The height of your potential is predicted by the people who surround you.' Achor differentiates between small potential, which we can reach by ourselves; and big potential, which we can reach with the help of others. Would Usain Bolt have been the fastest man on the planet if he had trained his whole life in isolation? Of course not. He had a coach, a strength coach, a technical director, his manager, the general secretary, training partners, family and friends, all of whom helped him in his pursuit of his potential.

We've looked so far at growth and engagement on an individual level. Here we examine the increased happiness of individuals and the team in a high-functioning, collaborative environment.

WHAT HAPPENS IF WE DON'T COLLABORATE?

In 1999 French naval officials were celebrating the launch of France's first ever nuclear-powered aircraft carrier, the *Charles de Gaulle,* which cost £2 billion and took ten years to build. Their celebrations were short-lived. Shortly after the fanfare had died down, it transpired that there was a critical flaw with the design. The deck of the carrier – pretty essential for aircraft taking off and landing – was 12 feet too short.

The planes France had purchased to use on their nuclear mega boat didn't exist in 1989, when the aircraft carrier was designed, meaning it had been designed for planes with a different landing specification. Looking at it the other way round: when the purchasing team were buying planes, they hadn't considered the crucial length of the aircraft's landing deck. They had failed to collaborate.

There are several reasons why collaboration doesn't happen, for example:

- One or both parties don't see the benefit.
- People have tried to collaborate, but their input has been ignored.
- People are afraid of being wrong or don't trust their teammates.
- People prefer to keep information to themselves for their own personal gain.

When we fail to collaborate well with our colleagues, we are creating bigger issues than we might imagine. In his TED Talk 'As work gets more complex, 6 rules to simplify', Yves Morieux explains that lack of cooperation leads to more time, more equipment, more systems, more rules and more teams – none of which leaders, shareholders or customers will pay for. Therefore, the cost of poor cooperation falls on the employees, who burn out, are unduly stressed and become overwhelmed.

Lack of collaboration forces organisations to use other methods with which to operate – metrics, processes, tick sheets, red tape, red tape, red tape. It makes more work for everyone. Collaboration offers the benefit of simplification and less bureaucracy. Ultimately, we are making our lives harder and therefore threatening our happiness and potential when we don't get teamwork right.

COMPETITION

Shawn Achor references a conversation with a Wall Street trader, who revelled in competition. When Shawn put forward his Big Potential theory, the trader asked why in the world Shawn might 'want to help someone else become more competitive. Isn't it better to be the smartest or strongest person in the room?' This quote epitomises a mindset abundant in businesses. While employees may not publicly shun the idea of working collaboratively, status-orientated, draconian avarice rumbles on unchallenged – and is sometimes even sanctioned – by leaders.

Competition is particularly useful for growth. However, there appears to be an interpretation of competition in the business setting that spills over into a Machiavellian world, where winning is winning at any cost and sometimes includes deceptive, underhand, immoral or unscrupulous behaviour.

We need the right kind of competition.

A desirable attitude to competition is described by Peter Haberl, a sport psychologist with the US Olympic Committee. He describes the two components to a winning attitude:

1. A desire to win, which is an external driver
2. A desire to perform at our best, which is internal

Olympic athletes want to win medals, but Haberl explains that, when the competition starts, the greatest Olympians focus on their best performance. After all, they cannot control the outcome of the race or their competitors' performance – they can only control how well they compete.

It's deeper and richer to reframe competition as competing with yourself, using other people as inspiration. It also bodes well not to confuse striving for excellence with winning. Winning might feel nice for a moment, but if you won a competition where no one properly challenged you, what did you gain from it?

Some workplaces are plagued by the winning-at-any-cost mentality and the need to squash others down to satiate a need for self-worth. But this feeling of greatness and recognition is short-lived. The way to succeed in a wholesome, sustainable way is to enjoy the fun and benefit of collaboration with others, not to fight against it.

Businesses need to think differently about supporting an individualistic, dog-eat-dog culture, in the understanding that they are not only contributing to disengagement, thus diminishing their returns, but also limiting everyone's potential.

COMPOSITION OF A SUCCESSFUL TEAM

Putting together all the highest performers results in a seething mass of clashing egos. Creating the best team is not as simple as selecting the best people at each level. Conversely, placing top performers with too many junior members of staff will not offer enough reciprocity of learning and motivation.

A great experiment was conducted by William Muir, a biologist from Purdue University, who observed the effects of team productivity by setting up an experiment with chickens. Chickens' productivity – the number of eggs they lay – is easy to measure. Muir selected one group of average chickens and one group of highest-productivity chickens and placed them in separate coops (or teams). After six generations, the average group were healthy and fully feathered, and their egg productivity had increased. Meanwhile, in the highest-productivity group, only three pretty dishevelled-looking chickens remained. The others had literally pecked each other to death.

Many analogise Muir's biological experiment to explain the behaviour in many businesses. Top performers might bully or forsake others until they reach the top, their success achieved by (figuratively) pecking the competition into submission, leaving the workplace a disparate, unhealthy place to be. This behaviour may not be obvious – it can present itself in little pecks of egotistical behaviour, negative, insensitive or passive-aggressive comments rather than in an almighty, overt attack.

In the Bruce Daisley podcast, 'The Culture of Teams', Mark de Rond, Professor of Organizational Ethnography at Cambridge University, writes about the team composition and teams acting under pressure. He describes how, when working with the Cambridge Boat Race team in 2007, they faced the difficult task of selecting the final eight rowers from a pool of 40. He explains that the challenge of creating the fastest boat arose through a mixture of technical competence and social competence. Five of the returning Blues from the previous year fought to have a particular oarsman in the boat, despite it being evident that he was not the best. He had a magic that allowed the team to dig deeper collectively, which was more valuable to them than selecting technically the best oarsmen.

In the same year, the Cambridge boat changed their coxswain only days before the race. They replaced the 2006 coxswain and Beijing Olympic hopeful, Russell Glenn, with Rebecca Dowbiggin, who had never taken part in competitive sport until arriving at Cambridge. Her selection was justified by the crew's need for a calming and relaxing cox. Cambridge won the 2007 Boat Race by a length.

We must recognise that the personal attributes of team members influence the success of a team or organisation overall, even if they don't muster the best results individually. But if we don't measure or prioritise personal attributes as part of our formula in composing a team, how will we determine the best mix? The examples above relied on feedback from the team members to support those who would probably have been overlooked. In the workplace, how often do we ask our teams who they would like to work with?

Let's not underestimate the person who brings unity, positivity, humour, fun or calm – they might just have the magic sauce that binds people together on a whole new level of happiness and success.

These examples beg the question: what are the ingredients for the perfect team?

THE PERFECT TEAM

In 2012 Google launched Project Aristotle, to study 180 teams within the company. They were looking for patterns to determine how they could compose the most successful teams. They looked at people's individual strengths such as intelligence, work ethic and resilience, and studied many other individual performance indicators, but they couldn't correlate which of those traits led to the most successful team. The researchers found that what really mattered was less about *who* is on the team and more about *how the team worked together.*

The key differentiator was that the most successful teams had psychological safety.

> **Teams with psychological safety think it's okay – even great – to raise ideas, concerns, mistakes and observations, all with the conviction that speaking up won't result in negative consequences.**

Amy Edmondson, American scholar of leadership and expert in psychological safety, discusses her initial PhD research in her TED Talk, 'Building a psychologically safe workplace'.

Edmondson was researching the relationship between error making and teamwork in hospitals. She expected to find that the most effective teams made fewer mistakes, but she actually found the opposite: teams who reported better teamwork were making more errors. When she dug into the data, she hypothesised that the best teams are not actually those *making* the most errors, but instead they are the teams who are more comfortable *reporting* the most errors. Reporting errors gave the team the best opportunity to discuss problems and find solutions.

If psychological safety is a key component to great teams, how do we get it?

PSYCHOLOGICAL SAFETY

Teams that feel comfortable expressing ideas, concerns, feelings and errors have managed to overcome some innate human behaviours. We enjoy building our self-esteem, so many of us work hard to avoid looking ignorant, inferior, silly or negative. However, psychologically safe teams don't worry about that. Psychologically safe is manifested in many small behaviours and interactions, but at its heart are trust and vulnerability.

Reliability

Every time we don't meet commitments, we erode trust. A good exercise to evaluate your reliability is to think about a time when you failed to meet a commitment. Ask yourself:

Was I reliable?

Can I count on myself to do what I commit to do?

If not, why not?

Alternatively, you could reflect generally on your reliability and score yourself on a scale of 1 to 5, before asking for feedback and examples from team members. This will give you a balanced review of what you see and what others experience.

Queen's Hospital

In 2017 I had an employee working for me who, on a personal level, I genuinely liked. He was enthusiastic, he worked pretty hard, and I envied his free-spiritedness and confidence.

He was generally doing well at work but then started behaving erratically, turning up late for work, sometimes not turning up at all. I had many conversations with him, trying to get to the bottom of what was going on, and he eventually confided in me that his drug use was getting out of control.

Drug use isn't that uncommon amongst 20-years-olds with some disposable income, so this wasn't a great surprise. We talked through it, and a big part of our conversation was that, once he had got himself straight, we'd need to work on our relationship to rebuild trust. He had previously used a series of rather unbelievable excuses for why he hadn't been turning up to work.

A couple of months later, he appeared to be back on the straight and narrow, and I felt hopeful things were on the up. When I received a text message saying that his grandma had been taken into hospital and he couldn't come to work, my doubts resurfaced. Still, I responded sympathetically but asked if he would send me a photo of where he was. He sent me a photo of the outside of Queen's Hospital in Romford ... a stock image I managed to find on Google within less than a minute.

I asked him to send me a photo of him in the hospital, with him in it. I was tempted to request that he should be holding a copy of that day's newspaper. He argued at first that using his mobile was against the hospital rules ... but eventually fessed up to his deception, and we agreed to part ways.

The vault

The vault is a term popularised by Brené Brown in her book *Dare to Lead*. One of the challenges of communication is sharing the right information, with the right person at the right time. The vault is a place where we keep what's not ours to share. It may not be our information to share at all, someone may not be the right person to share it with, or it might not be an appropriate time to share it.

Managers and leaders are frequently asked questions by their teams, and it is tempting to immediately give people the answer they seek. It's wiser, however, to use our emotional intelligence and self-control to check whether this is something that is ours to share in that moment, and with that person, or if it should stay in our vault for a later date. This doesn't mean we are lying to people. We can simply explain that we believe there is some discussion going on about the subject at the moment, but that it isn't our information to share at this time.

This applies to gossip too. Gossiping can feel good as it can build social bonds. Dislikes shared between groups of people are more powerful for human bonding than shared likes and other positive information, not to mention the thrill that can be achieved by divulging confidential information. However, gossiping is one of the most toxic behaviours in businesses, and we must diminish it in the workplace.

If people behave reliably and can honour the vault, it goes a long way towards building trust. The more trust we build with others, the less threatened and the more psychologically safe we can feel.

Vulnerability

What other words spring to mind when we say *vulnerability?*

We ask this question in one of our workshops and, invariably, the word weak comes top of the list.

In bygone days, people who spoke openly about insecurities and feelings were considered weak. Over the past decade, coaches of sports teams, progressive leaders and figures of state have been sounding more and more like pastoral carers. This is because they are *embracing* vulnerability.

Vulnerability is not weakness. It doesn't mean we need to cry or get overemotional. It also doesn't mean oversharing – no one needs to know salacious details that aren't appropriate to the workplace.

> **Vulnerability is when, at an appropriate moment, you share some things that you don't share often. It means you are okay with letting other people know you are fallible.**

This is about simple admissions such as:

- *I made a mistake.*
- *I got that wrong.*
- *I don't know anything about this.*
- *I'm out of my comfort zone.*
- *I'm finding this hard.*
- *I wish I had done that differently.*
- *I messed up with my client.*

We have existed for many decades throwing praise at infallible leaders, mirroring their stoic behaviour and aspiring to their unquestionable knowledge. Now everyone's starting to realise that that kind of leadership is all a bit of a myth. No one is actually infallible. Everyone has emotions and sometimes feels helpless, and no one knows everything. The leaders who masquerade as if they do will also make mistakes, such as hideous, unfiltered claims suggesting people try injecting bleach to conquer Covid. Admitting our knowledge limitations is very healthy for ourselves and for others.

I was a leader who had been taught to be strong and resilient according to the old-fashioned definition. I thought I needed to exude a persona of infallibility, so I rarely shared any of my errors with employees or indeed insights into my rather more entertaining home life.

The cone funnel

One day I confessed to our senior management team that I'd had an incident on the train on the way home from a Christmas lunch with them the previous year. I felt embarrassed and ashamed, and it took me a year to tell them about the incident because it didn't uphold the image I wanted to present of myself.

That day, though, I confessed about how I had fallen asleep on the train on the way home, after six hours trying to keep up on drinks with an 17-stone rugby player and a 28-year-old whippet. When I woke up, I instantly had that uneasy feeling and searched around for a bag in case I needed to barf. Aside from my handbag, there was nothing within reach other than the *Evening Standard* on my lap. I hastily fashioned the newspaper into a cone before vomiting into it, desperately trying to be discreet. Unfortunately, I had failed to connect the cone at the bottom, which created a funnel of puke onto the floor of the train. Shortly after, there was not only a pool of sick next to my seat but also a stream making its way down the centre of the train. I was wearing a rather loud, yellow dress that day and couldn't help feeling I was doing everything to draw attention to myself. I never wore the same outfit again, for fear of being recognised by fellow commuters.

To top it all off, my parents arrived from Edinburgh to stay for Christmas that day, so they were greeted by a confused, blubbering wreck, agonising over the shame of being a 37-year-old train vomiter. My mum simply said 'Merry Christmas' and let me sob on her shoulder.

The response from the management team when I told them this story? They loved it. They felt vindicated from their own similar exploits and liked that I was human, after all. I had been holding them at arm's length, which had of course been reciprocated. I recognise now that it felt powerful to pretend to be an infallible leader, but it felt much more fulfilling to admit to an embarrassing episode, break down the formal barriers and connect properly with this lovely team.

It took telling this anecdote for me to learn that we feel a much stronger connection with people when they share similar attributes or values, as well as their successes and failures. Employees will only really know and connect with their leader if their leader lets them in.

We might still be in the habit of concealing our fallibility, but we all know it's there – in others as much as in ourselves. And the feeling of acceptance, support and self-worth that can arise when we admit to feeling vulnerable is one of the most positive feelings we can generate with our team members.

Vulnerability doesn't diminish our ability to demonstrate resilience, determination, forthrightness and strength. Vulnerability just gives you more options to stretch and use all of your humanness. We can get rid of the peacocking, the stiff upper lip, the distance and the imperviousness. We're saying that you're allowed, and will benefit from, mixing it up.

In the TV series *Ted Lasso*, there's a scene where Ted, the manager of AFC Richmond, confides to his four colleagues that he has been suffering panic attacks. It has taken strength for him to share this, and the pattern of behaviour it invokes is a great example of how vulnerability creates psychological safety. The rest of the management team take turns in admitting things they wouldn't ordinarily have shared, from confessions of failed player signings to admitting to being high during one of the games, all because of the example set by Ted. And their confessions are met with sensitivity, gentle nods of acknowledgement and acceptance.

It can be tough to establish a culture of vulnerability, but two elements are essential to do so:

1. **Leading by example**

   If the leader can start to make tiny moves towards sharing more of their feelings, or concerns or truths about themselves, this will set permission for others to do the same. This doesn't have to be a coordinated exercise, though there are great team exercises on vulnerability available.

2. **Acceptance**

    When someone offers something with complete vulnerability, it is imperative that they are met with acceptance and curiosity and never with judgement or disdain. There is no quicker way to ruin psychological safety than a thoughtless eye roll or insensitive words in response to someone's vulnerable admission.

We no longer want or need our leaders to appear flawless. We want strength, positivity and determination, but we also yearn for humility, care and empathy. We want someone who can admit to mistakes and improve on their actions, especially as that's what's asked of employees. Leaders who show their fallibility, their vulnerability and their concern give employees the gift of being comfortable with theirs.

The swaggering, dispassionate leader does not foster psychological safety. The caring, trusting and humanly flawed one does. More vomiting stories from everyone, I say.

CHAPTER SUMMARY

A phrase popularised by John F Kennedy states that a rising tide lifts all boats. I translate this analogy to teamwork being the rising tide and everyone benefitting from their boat being lifted.

It is possible to do great things as an individual, but so much more can be accomplished when we collaborate as a team. We can eliminate more errors. We can create better innovations. We can provide, fun, inspiration and healthy competition for each other.

KEY REMINDERS FROM THIS CHAPTER

- Competition is healthy, especially when helping us reach our potential and helping businesses to grow. A personal, internal competition of excellence, using rivals and role models as inspiration, is a healthier competition to be in.
- The composition of a successful team requires technical performers and those who bring the magic sauce to the team. The attributes of fun, creativity, humility, communication and love are harder to evaluate, but that doesn't mean they are of less importance.

- The perfect team is about how the team works together, not just about the abilities of each team member.
- There's a popular saying that trust takes years to build, seconds to break and forever to repair. If we think about it this way, we might treat it differently.
- Creating psychological safety in our teams and establishing the closeness of relationships, where we can speak freely, is available to all of us. It requires a shift in behaviour, little by little.
- At work we are all ultimately performing for an audience, but this doesn't mean anyone needs to put on an act. Employees want to be genuinely themselves and work for genuine leaders. Embracing our humanness and vulnerability in the workplace creates closer teams.

CHAPTER 11

MORALITY, ACCOUNTABILITY AND ETHICS

MORALITY

In 2003 19-year-old Elisabeth Holmes dropped out of Stanford University and founded Theranos, a health technology company revolutionising the blood-testing market. Theranos had created breakthrough technology, which could perform blood tests using only a fraction of the blood required for usual tests, making the process much quicker and more cost-effective. Holmes attracted US $400 million from investors and venture capitalists, and the business was valued at $10 billion at its peak in 2013.

The emergence of Theranos came only two years after the demise of Enron, the formerly revered energy and trading business, which was once the seventh biggest business in America. Enron was founded in 1985 and generated revenues of over US $100 billion in 2000 (according to their questionable accounts), employing around 30,000 people worldwide.

What these two businesses have in common? Their success was based on fraud.

In the case of Theranos, the fraud continued for 12 years, until 2015, when John Carreyou of *The Wall Street Journal*, coupled with two medical professors who doubted the clinical claims of the technology, exposed the scandal. Theranos technology had been producing widely inaccurate results with their own machines, and they had been using technology approved by the FDA (Food and Drug Administration) from other manufacturers to pass off results as their own.

Elisabeth Holmes, who by 2015 had been lauded in *Fortune, Forbes* and *The New York Times Style Magazine*, promptly saw her personal net worth of US $4.5 billion plummet. In January 2022 she was convicted of defrauding investors.

Enron was in business for 16 years before their transgressions were uncovered and their fraudulent accounting activity, their narcissistic and untouchable leadership, and their cultural cesspit came back to bite them. They swiftly went into administration, dragging other offenders such as Arthur Andersen down with them.

Research carried out by Alexander Dyck, Adair Morse and Luigi Zingales, after the demise of Arthur Andersen in the Enron scandal, led them to speculate that, statistically, during the period of 1996 to 2004, one out of seven publicly listed companies was engaged in fraud (detected or undetected). Their report 'How pervasive is corporate fraud?' showed that firms in the US that engage in fraud destroy on average a fifth of their value – an estimated cost of US $380 billion a year. While this study was carried out in the US, there's no reason its findings wouldn't be indicative of the behaviour in other countries too.

The performance results of Enron and Theranos were so seductive for stakeholders and executives that no one wanted to question whether the success was legitimate. No one wanted to kill the goose that laid the golden egg. The behaviour and practices within the businesses were therefore condoned, overlooked and hidden, all in the name of results and wealth.

Many leaders hold themselves accountable for results but not behaviour.

The top of the tree is one of the most and least morally accountable places we can be. As people enjoy success, egos can inflate, heads can swell, and a sense of Machiavellian power and immunity can develop. It's this arrogance and untouchability that undoubtedly contributed to the behaviour exhibited by the leaders of Theranos and Enron. The CEO of Enron, Jeff Skilling, frequently celebrated his over-inflated ego and boasted of the company's success, all the while operating through a web of deceit and lies.

Accountability of private business owners is often the trickiest, as there's no one they are technically accountable to – no one can terminate their employment if their moral compass goes askew. Employees may leave, though it is startling how long Theranos and Enron employees looked past the clear fraud that was happening in front of them, and that they were perpetrating.

Of course, sometimes employees feel unable to raise poor behaviour with their leaders, due to their deference to authority and the fear of biting off the hand that feeds them. Next we look at how institutionalised we can become to a culture.

INSTITUTIONALISATION

In 1997 Korean Air Flight 801 crashed into a hill on its approach to Guam airport. 223 people were killed. Along with a series of misfortunes such as bad weather and outdated charts, Malcolm Gladwell argues, in his book *Outliers*, that one of the key contributors to the disaster of flight 801 was the Korean culture of hierarchy. The more junior co-pilot was afraid to question the poor judgement of the pilot, even as they were careering towards catastrophe.

The Theranos and Enron scandals also illustrate a fear of hierarchy, where the fraudulent practices in both businesses were evident to many employees. In the case of Theranos, it was a journalist who uncovered the fraud, not an employee. In the case of Enron, the fraudulent accounting practices and corruption were rife for years before they were brought to light by whistleblower Sherron Watkins, Enron's vice president.

The pressure on employees in these situations must be terrible. They not only fear for their own jobs if they speak up; they also fear the effect the information will have on the livelihoods of others who might be affected by the business's demise. Culturally, it's disrupting a tribe – one within which people are likely happy and secure.

Enron apparently sought legal advice on firing Sherron Watkins after she sent her infamous memo to the Enron board, in which she outlined her concerns about their creative accountancy methods. She still maintains that she is the 'only whistleblower in any kind of modern history that has a positive story', because Enron collapsed before they had a chance to see through any of their vengeful plans.

Companies can necessitate a culture of moral wrong doing. Wildly unachievable performance targets can drive people to dangerous levels, where their own morality becomes clouded and they forget where their boundaries are.

Employees and leaders can forget many of their own values and integrity as they become institutionalised to their environment. We eventually accept behaviour and conditions that we may originally have questioned – a state that psychologist Martin Seligman calls *learned helplessness.*

Seligman's ground-breaking study was based on dogs that were placed in crates with two compartments. One side of the crate would emit an electric shock at random, and the dogs quickly learned to jump to the other side to avoid receiving the shocks. However, the dogs that had experienced a prior test, in which they had been unable to avoid electric shocks, didn't look for a solution; they simply lay down, effectively conceding defeat and accepting that nothing could improve or change their situation.

Thankfully, no one has introduced electric shocks for employees (as far as I know), but when people experience stressful situations repeatedly, they build the belief that they are unable to control or change the situation, even when the opportunity for change becomes available.

Culture is constantly evolving, so we humans are trained to move and shape our behaviour in accordance with who and what we find around us. We learn from what we see our peers doing and we follow suit – we want to be part of the tribe. It takes significant clarity of thought, self-worth and courage to speak up when we notice a culture or person perpetuating learned helplessness. By speaking to those around us, particularly those disconnected from our work, we can start to look objectively at the circumstances and behaviour around us, and rationalise whether it still follows our personal moral code.

While the majority of transgressions don't reach serious criminal levels, they are a stark reminder of how quickly amoral behaviour can become commonplace.

THE DICHOTOMY OF DECISIONS

Morality, in simplistic terms, becomes cognitively challenging when we place it into real scenarios. For example:

- Should someone break the speed limit to reach hospital quickly with an injured patient if this endangers the lives of other road users?
- If you see someone drowning in a strong current, should you try and save them if you'd be risking your own life?

Workplace happiness is affected by subjective perception of right and wrong, and it causes employees to lament over what is fair and what is unfair.

If leaders suspect they may have to close an office and make a number of redundancies, would it be morally right to immediately share this information with those who might be affected? If they do, the employees at risk of redundancy could more quickly find alternative work. However, if too many people chose to leave at this point, it could disrupt the remaining business. If leaders withhold this information until they have had a chance to interrogate it fully, consider options and make informed decisions, they will gain time to help safeguard the rest of business. However, they might then be jeopardising the financial security of the employees who will ultimately lose their jobs.

Which is right? Welcome to the dichotomy of decisions.

Hiring excellent talent into a business is good because high performers raise the bar for everyone. Win-win. However, what if an excellent person needed £10,000 more on their basic salary than an employee currently in the same role? Should the company stick to strict salary bands? This way, they will maintain fairness but may never raise the bar beyond their current best performer. Or should they speculate that this new individual is worth the extra salary and hope others don't find out? If that works well, the whole team can learn from the new employee, and the performance of the entire company will improve. If it's the wrong call, there will no doubt be calamitous consequences on the team morale and on others' salary expectations. It's simpler to put salaries up, but incredibly difficult to bring them down. What's the 'right' decision?

In some form, we will all have witnessed or been part of similar dilemmas in the workplace, which are rarely as binary as right and wrong. Decisions like this can also often be confidential, so employees may draw incorrect or incomplete conclusions.

Here are some tips for overcoming the dichotomy of decisions:

- We can help create happier employment if we start with a baseline of *assuming positive intent.* There is nearly always justification for any decision or action.
- Leaders should, wherever possible, illustrate the factors any decision has been based on.

- In a situation with no clear right or wrong, employees and leaders must have faith in each other to make the best call they can.
- We must accept that a misjudgement doesn't warrant blame. Where someone has made a poor decision, they should demonstrate accountability, acknowledge their actions and decisions, and put it right.

ACCOUNTABILITY

Being accountable is about owning our actions and our mistakes – it's the opposite of blame. Would behavioural transgressions occur less frequently if we held ourselves and each other more accountable?

PEER-TO-PEER ACCOUNTABILITY

Peer groups find it challenging to hold each other to account due to *interpersonal discomfort*, a term coined by Patrick Lencioni in his book, *The Five Dysfunctions of a Team*. It refers to the feeling that equals are uncomfortable holding each other to account for their actions or behaviour; why would someone be qualified to point out to an equal how to do their job?

In sport, teammates regularly alert each other when they need to be held to account, for example:

Midfield, track back!
Mark number 6!
Watch your left shoulder!

It's helpful – a player can't see the whole pitch, so others can point to things they have missed or help when players are committed elsewhere. There is little interpersonal discomfort within sports teams. Culturally, teammates perceive pointers as helpful rather than belittling; and the common goal – winning the game – is more important than individual performance.

Teams in the workplace often do the opposite, prioritising comfort or status over and above the common goal. The successful performance of the business becomes secondary to individual preferences. This individual need for status and comfort prevents honest conversations, where team members could hold each other to account.

A hockey player on my team once told me how and why a goal scored by the opposition was my fault. She wasn't blaming me – she was educating me. The feedback hurt a bit, but I damn sure didn't let anyone cut back inside me again. I hate to think how many more goals I would have been accountable for if my teammate hadn't told me what I'd missed that time.

The takeaway here: no matter how hard it feels to hold each other to account, the outcome will almost certainly be worse if we don't. It won't normally be as bad the criminal fraud of Enron and Theranos, but it could be significant. It could be bullying, harassment, unhappiness or burnout. We can't expect only leaders and managers to hold employees accountable for behaviour – they often only see a fraction of what's happening.

PERSONAL INTEGRITY

It's easiest to neglect our own behaviour when no one is watching. We've all probably helped ourselves to others' juice or milk when no one was looking but would have refrain from doing so if anyone had been there to witness it; we care what people think of our behaviour. As John Wooden said, 'The true test of a man's character is what he does when no one is watching.'

On my way to work, I sometimes can't help earwigging into others' conversations. It recently struck me how slanderous many of those idle chats are, and how distressed the targets would feel if they were sitting in my seat. If you listen out, you might notice the pervasiveness of these conversations yourself.

In his TED Talk 'Why it's so hard to make healthy decisions', behavioural economist David Asch describes a fascinating study, which took place in an intensive care unit in a Florida Hospital, where the handwashing rates had been lamentably low. Researchers simply put a photograph of someone's eyes above the sink, to give the impression that anyone near the sink was being watched. Handwashing rates more than doubled. We perform better even when we *imagine* we are being observed.

Where would you put eyes on yourself to improve your own behaviour? Perhaps you know that you tend to have gossipy conversations with colleagues around the water cooler, criticising management or the company. Now imagine your managers were listening. Similarly, managers or leaders who vent frustrations about their teams should remind themselves to think, *What if that team member were listening?*

Shouldn't we all alter our comments to be more objective and respectful? Isn't that a good thing?

ETHICS

In their paper 'Ethical Fading: The Role of Self-Deception in Unethical Behavior', Ann Tenbrunsel and David Messick coined the term *ethical fading*, which refers to the erosion of ethical standards. This erosion often begins with something benign – employees or leaders convincing themselves that what they are doing isn't *too* wrong, that it's justified or that it won't affect others badly. Two small examples of ethical transgression, which still break the rules:

- Searching for holidays online during work hours
- Checking social media throughout the workday

We are all guilty of telling ourselves a story, based on our own subjective narrative, to assess whether behaviour is acceptable. For example:

- *I work so hard for the company, they should allow me some time here and there to find a holiday.*
- *No one has noticed and I can still get my job done, so what's wrong with me using my work time for personal things?*

What would that employee say if a colleague took it a step further and used an entire day to search online for their holiday – is that too much? Or is the disparity of time between those that spend only a few minutes versus those that spend longer now actually unfair? Where does it stop?

Keeping a tacit mental tally of how hard we feel we are working, versus what we feel the company owes us, is a dangerous approach. However, it's what most of us – leaders and employees – do. The only person aware of the facts is you, and it's easy to reason out those facts to suit our own narrative.

The unadulterated truth is that we are paid to work during work hours, but businesses that take exception to these small transgressions might be deemed harsh, inflexible and untrusting. However, could businesses that condone this type of activity be endorsing ethical breaches and inviting further, more serious breaches?

The main difficulty with small ethical transgressions is that they can turn into bigger ones, while we continue to justify their worth.

Ethical fading spirals when a culture of unethical behaviour develops.

In June 2000 California suffered an electricity crisis and endured two days of rolling blackouts, which affected businesses and public services as well as much of everyday life in California. It later transpired that Enron, then a wholesaler of electricity to California, had been deliberately restricting supply because this shortage enabled them to sell their electricity on to retail suppliers at over 20 times the price. A few years after the demise of Enron, recordings of phone conversations surfaced in which traders had discussed and planned this market manipulation.

Why did the traders lose their moral compass? The manipulation likely started out small and was rationalised as essential to deliver results for Jeff Skilling, Enron's president at that time, who had told them to trade aggressively in California and take advantage of the partially deregulated wholesale market. Once you have crossed the line and then see others crossing the line, it starts to become part of the culture. I have no doubt that the ethical fading also persisted because of the significant profit gain for Enron and monetary gain for its traders. Their own gain clouded their ethical judgement – so much so that this went on for over a year.

There should be discussion in every business on where ethical lines are drawn; and on how to find the balance of freedom, within guidelines that prevent innocuous transgressions becoming unacceptable.

HONESTY AND TRUST

We have all probably been asked to trust someone in the past, and this trust has frequently been honoured. However, much like when my son asked me to trust him that he wouldn't eat any more sweets, it can be easy to succumb to temptation, or to underestimate the importance of what's been promised.

The UK public are amongst the most trusting globally, a 2023 survey by Kings College London discovered. This might feel surprising, with the number of crime statistics gleefully reported in our press. The research, however, states that less than half – 46% – of Brits reckon most people are trustworthy.

On my way

A colleague of mine used to recruit for trades positions on construction sites and had spent a couple of days chasing up one particular chippie, Steve, who had been turning up late to site. Eventually, after another complaint from the site manager, my colleague decided to try and find out what was going on.

When he finally reached him on the phone, Steve waxed lyrical about train disruptions and what a nightmare of a journey he'd had, but said he was now on his way and was walking towards the site. In fact, he said, he was so close that he could already see the hoarding and site office.

My colleague said, 'Steve … I called you on your landline.'

When we uncover dishonesties, we of course lose trust.

I have been trolled, had my database stolen and been verbally abused and threatened. I have had to terminate the employment of several people for stealing property and money from my businesses. I have also known people I had completely trusted commit the most awful deceptions. Employment really can show up the worst in people.

While managers and leaders recognise that those who are dishonest are often in a tiny minority, the volume of negative experiences can compound into a cynical perspective.

A cynical perspective is difficult to confine to the offending individuals, and leaders can start to feel they can't trust their whole team, even starting to work defensively to protect themselves from further disappointment. The impact of this is huge: leaders will be demotivated. Their morale and performance is integral to the performance of the team and the company, so everyone's potential will suffer.

A lack of trust can also significantly impact policy making. In an era where flexible working and working from home are increasingly sought-after, leaders jaded by the dishonest behaviour of the minority may feel compelled to reduce freedom to try to curb dishonesty.

Leaders can of course be dishonest too. I have seen the scenario where leaders try to entice a new employee on board with the promise of a certain goal in the future, which they may have no real intention of seeing through.

Honesty at work is a tricky subject. No company or team member is ever *completely* honest in the workplace, nor should they be, because sometimes honesty is unnecessarily hurtful and unproductive. We should, however, be caring and direct, selfless and compassionate. And we should take great care to behave according to our morals, ethics and integrity.

CHAPTER SUMMARY

Results matter, and so does method. If you end up more successful than you had ever imagined, you also want to be proud of the behaviour that got you there.

We have seen, through the examples of ethical fading, that just about anyone in the everyday workplace can have slightly dubious moral and ethical tendencies. This will hopefully humble our sense of righteousness and encourage us all to understand that right and wrong aren't always clear-cut.

We must take care to respect boundaries and to maintain a moral compass that allows for some justification of indiscretions. Leaders must take care to create cultures that afford enough adult freedoms, and environments that don't entice ethical fading.

KEY REMINDERS FROM THIS CHAPTER

- Check in on your moral compass. Just because behaviour is condoned or overlooked, that doesn't mean it's okay.
- Use your own integrity to decide whether you are behaving in accordance with your own personal values. Change anything that needs changing, and bear integrity in mind whenever a decision challenges it.
- We all do better when we are held to account. Peers can hold each other to account, regardless of levels and status. Feedback is essential to growth, and it doesn't matter who it comes from. A culture without accountability breeds apathy and poor standards.

- No decision is every going to be perfect for everyone, and the line between fair and unfair can be fuzzy. While we should err towards assuming positive intent, we also need to be confident to challenge decisions that don't sit right with us.

CHAPTER 12

WE'RE ALL IN THIS TOGETHER

> 'Speak ill of no man, but speak all the good you know of everybody.'
> – Benjamin Franklin

As children grow up, gain confidence and desire increasing levels of independence, their parents are faced with a higher potential of rebellion and must adapt, in individual ways, to their children's needs All the while, children will start to notice the fallibility of their parents and better understand the challenges of relinquishing control while also providing protection and guidance. This is mirrored in the workplace.

> **Much of modern employment still echoes a pseudo parent–child relationship.**

Leaders are custodians of those within their business. Employees are also custodians of their leaders. The employee–leader relationship is therefore bilateral, as is happiness.

While working collaboratively with a large group of people for a considerable amount of time can test everyone's resolve, leaders and employees recognising that their happiness is reciprocal will motivate deeper conversations and connections. We are all in this together.

From the start of the book, I have emphasised that *everyone* can create better opportunities and environments for happiness. This chapter gives a few additional aides-mémoires, separately for leaders and employees, by singling out specific challenges or frustrations from each.

Whether you are an employee or a leader, this chapter will remind you of how it feels to be in someone else's shoes and then use that empathy to create happier relationships and workplaces.

LEADERS

THE SELF-FULFILLING PROPHECY OF BELIEF

You are what you eat.

I think, therefore I am.

If you think you can or you think you can't, you're right.

All of these statements are self-fulfilling prophecies – things that become true by virtue of having been predicted or expected.

We've ruminated over belonging and esteem, over bias and judgement, and over the need for leaders to connect with those who are different from them. All of this culminates in the need for a self-fulfilling prophecy whereby leaders believe in their people.

> **Successful leaders believe in those they lead.**

> **Employees perform better under leaders who believe in them.**

Tired, stressed leaders can fall victim to negativity bias and be drawn to recognise people's faults more than their strengths. This happens frequently in our personal relationships too. Perhaps it's being British that makes some of us tend to orientate to what's wrong as opposed to what's right. We are after all, the nation that answers the question *How are you?* with *Not too bad.*

Losing belief in someone is a vicious circle. Employees and employers alike feel that loss of faith and lose confidence, and their performance suffers.

> **Leaders must fight unconscious negativity bias.**

When they think about or discuss one of their team members, leaders must learn to focus on the positive things about that person and their work. The effect of thinking or speaking positively about all team members is profound. Not only does it train the leader to start to see the positives more readily, but the leader also gains a reputation for positivity and believing in their team.

Belief mustn't be manufactured; it must be honest. This practice will therefore involve leaders searching for the positive elements they genuinely value. It might be harder to see those elements in some people than in others, but the positives are always there. If you struggle to see someone's positive attributes, ask other people for input – they will identify different values in that person. Only by offering employees belief will leaders create the best environment for employees to fulfil their potential.

LAZY LEADERSHIP

In *Reinventing Organizations*, Frederic Laloux talks about when French manufacturer FAVI discovered that one of their drills had been stolen from the factory. CEO Zobrist put up a flipchart in the stockroom, with a message stating what had happened and reinforcing that stealing anything in the business was a sackable offence. He then reiterated that the theft was simply stupid because anyone could have borrowed the company's tools.

What would happen if something at your workplace was stolen? Would a new system be introduced to monitor items being taken and put back into the stockroom? Would CCTV be installed? Would someone be assigned the task of monitoring the stockroom contents, stamping a ledger as items came in and out? Businesses are partial to tick sheets and moronic processes, because there's little a good process cannot solve … or so most leaders seem to believe.

This is what Simon Sinek, in his book *The Infinite Game*, terms *lazy leadership* – where leaders put efforts into building processes rather than improving trust and communication with their teams. The problems with some processes are as follows.

1. They do not address the root of the problem (trust in this instance).
2. They are often created with only a tiny minority of people in mind.
3. If employees can't see the value of a process, they will simply find a way around it that makes sense to them.

Stapling

When a friend of mine at a large law firm needed some more paperclips, she discovered she first had to send a requisition form to the head office in Leeds. She then waited 24 hours for the requisition to be signed off by the supply manager. After 48 hours, she was granted access to the stationery cupboard, which was about 30 steps away from her desk … by which time she'd used a stapler instead.

What feeling was she left with? After studying hard for seven years to become a lawyer, passing a tough interview process to gain employment at the firm and passing her first review with flying colours, she couldn't be trusted with the treasure trove that was the stationery cupboard. Some poor person probably also had to reconcile the cupboard's stock with the requisition forms at the end of each month.

I dread to think of the levels of paperclip theft there must previously have been within that organisation for such administrative nonsense to have been deemed necessary.

Senseless processes exasperate employees, to the point where they question the culture of the business. Pointless processes challenge the best employees the most, as they probably wouldn't do anything in contravention of best practice anyway.

Stop lazy leadership and replace it with clear messaging and guidance. And for god's sake, give your team as many paperclips as they need.

Let's emancipate employees. We can make it clear that there will be consequences for abusing trust and leave it like that. Employees will get it wrong, but probably with such infrequency that it's not worth losing sleep over or building another system for. How liberating for everyone.

PREFERENCES

Leaders can have a natural tendency to assess work based on how they would have done it or how they would have presented it. They should therefore take great care to distinguish between errors and preferences. Correcting errors facilitates learning. Applying preferences stifles autonomy.

LISTEN TO EMPLOYEES

A common criticism from employees is that they don't feel listened to. At other times, the leaders listen but either fail to take the employee's perspective fully into account, or make decisions without ample explanation.

> **Failing to listen to employees can have catastrophic consequences for businesses. Leaders must welcome feedback from their employees and treat it with respect.**

A perfect example of the consequences of failing to listen to employees is the 2010 Deepwater Horizon oil spill, the largest marine oil spill in history, in the Gulf of Mexico. An employee had warned executives that their plans to expand the well would increase the risk of leaks. His warnings were ignored ... and 4.9 million barrels of oil were spilled into the Gulf. This remains one of the worst environmental disasters in world history, in which 11 rig workers lost their lives.

WHAT'S YOUR LEGACY?

Thinking retrospectively can shape our thoughts differently. While a little morbid, an excellent question for leaders to ask themselves often is what people will be saying about them after they've left this mortal coil. Fundamentally, we all care about what other people think of us. If those thoughts were going to be stamped on our tombstones for eternity, we'd sharpen our focus on opting for admirable behaviour.

> **What is the impact you want your business to make on your employees, customers and community?**

I would imagine most leaders might prefer their business culture to be described as dignified, respectful, caring, passionate, successful, happy, meaningful, authentic and loyal, rather than autocratic, controlling, micromanaging, hypocritical, dispassionate, powerful or ruthless. Leaders who visualise how they want to make people feel, and who stay true to that vision, will make their desired impact on people and on the world.

To what extent are you living the legacy you aspire to? Visualise who you want to be. Write it down and develop the learning and actions you need to get there.

EMPLOYEES

Now let's turn our focus to how employees might learn to change and adapt in the workplace.

LEADERSHIP FATIGUE

Employees look to leadership to emulate the enthusiasm and positivity of a kids' entertainer, who has tricks up their sleeves, incentives, prizes and snacks, to lift spirits whenever needed. We have heard how contagious positivity is, and how important it is in the workplace, but what happens when the entertainer gets fatigued?

> **The fact that leaders are being paid more to fulfil their role doesn't make them immune to positivity fatigue. In fact, it probably makes their role emotionally more cumbersome.**

When we are worn down by workload, deadlines or pressures in and outside of work, as well as the burden of trying to inspire and motivate, we all react differently. Some people recoil into a cocoon, some become more irritable, and some publicly lose the plot.

Leading and managing people is an exhausting exercise. It's akin to organising a holiday with a large group of friends and trying to satisfy everyone's preferences for activities, accommodation, destinations and meals … and that's only for a week or two. Leaders and managers may not look exhausted, but they probably are. They too are complex humans with much going on in their lives outside of work.

Look around you. You'll be able to identify a manager who looks a bit flat, who is struggling, who is uncharacteristically snappy, whose attitude has soured, or who always works late. Now take some time out to make some small effort to help that person feel better. You'll be pleasantly surprised by how rewarding this feels, and your manager will love you for recognising their struggle.

While the manager's job description may decree that they must motivate their team, our happiness is interwoven with and dependent on each other. We are better as a team, and we accomplish more as a team, so each person taking a turn to carry the baton of happiness and positivity will help lift everyone's spirits and reduce the burden on leaders.

PERFECTLY HUMAN

We overtly discuss humans as wonderfully *imperfect* – their flaws and gaffs are the things that make them human. We openly acknowledge that we have our own weaknesses, and we accept that they are normal and exist in everyone. Despite this, there is still a high demand on companies to operate flawlessly.

The creation of a company as a legal entity seems to elevate expectations of perfection far beyond what individuals might expect of themselves and of each other outside of work. The dichotomy here is that companies are merely a collection of flawed individuals. The fact that they are working together as a group doesn't make them immune to making unpopular decisions or getting things wrong.

The Hull branch of Krispy Kreme doughnuts risked the company's reputation in just one online post. Publicising a half-term activity for kids, they unfortunately titled it 'Krispy Kreme Klub', shortened to KKK. Despite prompt apologies and removal of the post, they couldn't prevent the publicity sticking numerous posts of photoshopped Klu Klux Klan members enjoying Krispy Kreme doughnuts continued to appear.

Similarly, the album production and marketing team of Susan Boyle (runner-up of *Britain's Got Talent* in 2009), made an undignified Twitter gaff. The tweet read, 'Susan will be answering your questions at her exclusive album listening party on Saturday. Send in your questions #susanalbumparty Susan HQ'.

The hashtag was quickly changed, with capital letters inserted, but not before hordes of sniggering adults had latched on to the first tweet. While it's widely regarded that the gaff was intentional (the publicity helped generate 25 million album sales worldwide), these corporate blunders happen frequently and can have unfortunate outcomes.

Getting things perfectly right all the time is impossible, and leaders can't aspire to please everyone. Employees can help their leadership by pointing out errors or deficiencies directly to the leadership or management. If something has been screwed up, a strong leadership will rectify it. If a decision is unpopular, they will explain it. Employees can also help by remembering that their employer is as flawed as they are.

ASK FOR PRAISE

I know it may feel like showboating, but asking for praise is one of the biggest gifts you can give to your employer. It's often difficult for a manager or leader to see underneath the surface of results, and there's often a lot of behaviour and interactions they haven't seen or understood, which they would love to praise. Employees who don't receive adequate praise and recognition can become disengaged, so rather than labouring on without it, why not take a bolder step and ask for praise? It might feel uncomfortable at first, but factual statements like the examples below will soon become habitual.

I wanted to let you know that I offered [something] to a client, and they responded well. Perhaps that's something that we could roll out to others in the company?

I thought I would let you know that I spent an hour discussing the pros and cons of the new role with Michelle. I think it helped her to see the position in a more positive light.

I have been trying to get through to the company director for five months. This morning I succeeded, we had a good conversation, and we have set up a meeting for two weeks from now.

When I was outside yesterday, I overheard that Jasmine was a bit overwhelmed with her work, so Mike and I helped her with some urgent stuff and suggested she speak to her manager about her workload.

The manager would likely have had no idea of these situations. If we struggle on, bashfully hoping a manager will magically become aware of the extra effort we've made, we'll notch these achievements in our tacit tally of worthiness, all the while feeling frustrated. And our manager will probably never know about that either.

If this feels too much like blowing your own trumpet, find another way. Just don't let your own actions or those of your colleagues go unnoticed.

CHAPTER SUMMARY

I have attended many of our clients' company conferences, and I always ask the audience for their thoughts and observations of the presenters and the content. It is truly eye-opening to discover how differently people perceive and interpret what they have heard. Some people find one presenting style vastly favourable to another, while others in the same audience feel the exact opposite. Some people are left frustrated that a particular piece of information isn't mentioned, while others lament that there has been too much detail.

It is impossible to get employment perfectly right for everyone all the time. The multitude of different thoughts, opinions, biases, emotions, preferences, beliefs, values and priorities means that we are all always striving to accommodate each other. A constant appreciation of the fact that we are all so different, but that we ultimately all want the same thing, will motivate us to communicate better, refrain from judging each other, and support each other. This way we can all work towards achieving the one thing we all want in our work: happiness.

CONCLUSION

> 'Nobody made a greater mistake than he who did nothing because he could do only a little.'
> – Edmund Burke

I regularly fall down a rabbit hole of watching endless videos on Facebook of intensely happy or sad life stories of people I have never met. It never fails to surprise me how profoundly impacted I am by the situations of those I'm watching. I'm most affected by videos of babies or toddlers who are being fitted with cochlear implants, when I witness the joy as they hear something for the first time in their lives. The smiles, the giggles and the pure delight often bring me to tears.

I'm of course not alone in this. Most of us glean happiness from the happiness of others, and this is amplified when we have contributed to it. We have no reason to want anyone to be unhappy, and yet, despite knowing the reciprocal benefits, we don't always work hard on improving our colleagues' happiness.

Deep, lasting happiness is not truly fulfilled by witnessing happy events of people we don't know. These give us wonderful but temporary spikes, which we forget a few seconds later.

> **True happiness comes from interacting every day with people we care about in pursuit of something we care about.**

The workplace is full of people we care about. We may not have been vulnerable enough, self-aware enough, selfless enough or accepting enough to connect with them yet. Much of our unhappiness exists because we have misunderstood one another, have failed to be rational and objective, haven't talked to someone about how we feel, or haven't used the best language.

We don't have to like everyone we work with. However, caring about the happiness of everyone we work with, while investing in our relationships with them, is always worthwhile. After all, our own happiness and success at work depend on our colleagues' happiness and success.

Companies are human enterprises. They are therefore as flawed and imperfect as people, and often more so when imperfections are compounded through lack of diversity. Employees and leaders must come together and talk afresh about how to create a better understanding of each other and how to foster a culture that prioritises everyone's happiness.

Remember the formula: Happiness = productivity = success. Even if we find it difficult to bond with certain colleagues, we can still subscribe to the reciprocal benefit and contagiousness of happiness, and the success that comes with it.

GETTING ACTIVE ABOUT HAPPINESS

Adam Smith makes an interesting observation in *The Theory of Modern Sentiments*. He notes that, if there were a terrible tragedy on the other side of the world and thousands of people were killed, we would feel sorrow and think about how precious life is; but once we had done this, we would go about our lives as normal. Paradoxically, if we believed that someone would cut off one of our little fingers tomorrow, we would toss and turn all night with anxiety at our own paltry misfortune. Our fixation with our own troubles often surpasses our concern for others.

However, if we were given the choice of losing a little finger in order to save thousands of people on the other side of the world, none of us would blink before making our decision. Even if our passive thoughts are contemptible and selfish, our active thoughts are generous and noble. We aren't as selfish as we might think.

We frequently forget happiness in the workplace, while we are busy hitting targets, writing presentations, managing staff or running the factory line, all the while feeling pressure, tiredness and stress. We need to remember that other people's happiness is as important to them as ours is to us. We must retrain ourselves to consider our colleagues as individuals who want to experience happiness just as we do. In doing so, we can recognise our own impact on their wellbeing.

I know that people will have good days and bad, that employees' and leaders' behaviour will ebb and flow, and that enthusiasm and positivity will wax and wane. I know what a mountain there is to climb ahead of us, and when you go into work tomorrow, everything will probably look pretty much the same as it did yesterday. Something will be different, though. You will be different. You will have started to understand the importance of workplace happiness and the changes you can make to get on the road to improving it.

We must not allow our lives to return to the state where we ignore the injustices of unhappy employment. Now we know better, we have the choice to do better. We can bring more collective consciousness to the world about creating happier workplaces. Together, we can re-engineer employment into something that most of us cherish rather than endure. I, for one, want to ensure that my children grow into more evolved, inclusive, flexible and adult workplaces.

Businesses should aspire to their employees being there because they want to be, not because they have to be. Humanity has surely passed the point at which monitoring, supervising and controlling employees are the main productivity drivers in business.

Hopefully, the fact that there are employees who entirely self-manage successfully, who control and prioritise their own work, whose employers want them to enjoy authenticity and purpose at work, and who do so in adult relationships with their peers who were previously their managers, encourages you to ask yourself whether you want to be part of this revolution.

Men are moisturising with abandon and thriving as stay-at-home dads. Women are winning football tournaments and leading countries. White privilege and Black Lives Matter are now better acknowledged, and teenage eco-warriors are kicking politicians' asses. Traditional norms the world over are being disrupted, just as we are vocalising our need for a more sensitive, connected and caring culture, where everyone can be themselves inside of work and out. That sounds like a happier place, and we can get there, together.

ACKNOWLEDGEMENTS

There's no further new information from this point about creating happier employment so feel free to shut the book should you so choose. There follows, however, some examples of appreciation, which we heard about in Chapter 6, if you want to see it in action …

I appreciate my husband for his commitment to me and the time I needed to write. This book started as a passion project, and I'm not sure he or I (or anyone else, for that matter!) was really sure the text would ever see the light of day. It turned into a way to learn deeply about a subject matter that I found fascinating, which he backed with interest, time and support. He also read some of the early drafts and gave me feedback, suggesting I remove the swear words, so I stopped asking him to read it.

My kids. As the next generation, they were rather an inspiration for this book. I can vouch for the fact that developing your self-awareness of the behaviours that serve you – and those that don't – is particularly relevant to parenting. I appreciate my children for the glorious humans they are, and for putting up with the poorer moments of parenting I'm still trying to work on. Perhaps they can write Volume II in 20 years' time.

My business partner, Holly. Lordy, this woman has patience. Whether it's for the speed at which I talk, the crazy non-sequitur ideas that I throw into the mix, or for bearing with me talking about this book for nearly five years, she's a saviour. She is also good at finding passports that she/I may have thrown around a dingy bar in Bucharest after having too much tequila. And thanks also to Jacky T, another of the Condor Collective crew, who read and critiqued some early chapters. He was also the one who took us to the dingy bar in Bucharest so Holly and I hold him entirely responsible for my missing passport (and lost phone…).

My editor, Ilsa. Thank goodness there was someone involved in this project who actually has a command of English. Ilsa is relentlessly encouraging, and her ability to remember a book's content and hold enthusiasm for it, for more years than it takes to grow a 50-foot tree, is astonishing. She made me feel competent and purposeful and did more work on this book than I feel I have paid her for. She's a miracle worker. If you notice that this section is written less well than the rest of the book, it's because I have snuck it in after she has finished proofreading.

My brother. For reading the final draft. Well, he listened to it on audiobook while out walking his dog, so he admitted that some of his feedback made no sense as he couldn't remember what chapter it referred to. I can't remember why he told me to use James Milner in a story somewhere (I think just because he's a massive Liverpool fan) or why he suggested I include the famous quote from Shelley's 'Ozymandias' poem: 'My name is Ozymandias, king of kings: Look on my works, ye Mighty, and despair!' He couldn't remember either. I thank him for his input, even if I ignored chunks of it.

To my mum and dad. Mum, for reading a very early draft and meticulously correcting all the grammar in it. Unfortunately, I think I have rewritten the entire book since that point, but I thank her enormously for her time and dedication to my crap grammar. Dad, for asking with genuine enthusiasm when he will be able to read my book, despite the fact that he hates reading anything other than period drama novels and crime. The 'wokeness' of this book should also stimulate some interesting commentary from him. When this starts, I will know he has read it.

To the friends, neighbours, family and clients to whom I mentioned this book in 2018. The enthusiasm with which they repeatedly asked how the book was going was only trumped by their ability not to get bored of asking. This book is testament to the fact that if you don't set a deadline, it takes far longer to finish something than it is necessary to take.

REFERENCES

Achor et al., '9 Out of 10 People Are Willing to Earn Less Money to Do More-Meaningful Work', *Harvard Business Review*, 2018, https://hbr.org/2018/11/9-out-of-10-people-are-willing-to-earn-less-money-to-do-more-meaningful-work, accessed 25 September 2023

Achor, S, *Big Potential: Five Secrets of Reaching Higher by Powering Those Around You*, Virgin Books, 2018

Achor, S, *The Happiness Advantage*, Random House, 2011

Adkins, A, 'Only 35% of U.S. Managers Are Engaged in Their Jobs', Gallup, 2015, www.gallup.com/workplace/236552/managers-engaged-jobs.aspx, accessed 25 September 2023

Ariely, D, *Predictably Irrational* – The Hidden Forces That Shape Our Decisions, HarperCollins Publishers, 2008

Ariely, D, 'What makes us feel good about our work?', TED, 2013, www.ted.com/talks/dan_ariely_what_makes_us_feel_good_about_our_work, accessed 25 September 2023

Asch, D, 'Why it's so hard to make healthy decisions', TED, 2019, www.ted.com/talks/david_asch_why_it_s_so_hard_to_make_healthy_decisions, accessed 25 September 2023

Bakke, DW, *Joy at Work: A Revolutionary Approach To Fun on the Job*, Pear Press, 2016

Barton, D, 'Business Population Estimates for the UK and the Regions 2020', Department for Business, Energy & Industrial Strategy, 2020, www.gov.uk/government/statistics/business-population-estimates-2020/business-population-estimates-for-the-uk-and-regions-2020-statistical-release-html, accessed 25 September 2023

Boyle, D, *Steve Jobs*, Universal Pictures, 2015

Briceño, E, 'How to get better at the things you care about', TED, 2017, www.ted.com/talks/eduardo_briceno_how_to_get_better_at_the_things_you_care_about, accessed 25 September 2023

Chapman, G, *The Five Love Languages: How to Express Heartfelt Commitment to Your Mate*, Northfield Publishing, 1992

Collins, JC, *Good to Great: Why Some Companies Make the Leap…p and Others Don't*, HarperCollins, 2001

Craig JV, Muir, WM, 'Selection for Reduction of Beak-Inflicted Injuries Among Caged Hens', ScienceDirect, 1993, www.sciencedirect.com/science/article/pii/S0032579119338520, accessed 25 September 2023

Deloitte, 'Global Human Capital Trends 2016 – The new organization: Different by design', Deloitte, 2016, www2.deloitte.com/content/dam/Deloitte/global/Documents/HumanCapital/gx-dup-global-human-capital-trends-2016.pdf, accessed 25 September 2023

Dmukhovskaya, M, 'World Mental Health Day: Team USA psychologist Peter Haberl shares his secrets about how athletes' minds work', Olympics, 2021, https://olympics.com/en/news/the-team-behind-the-team-team-usa-psychologist-peter-haberl, accessed 25 September 2023

Duckworth, A, Grit: The Power of Passion and Perseverance, Scribner Book Company, 2016

Duckworth, A, '*Grit: The power of passion and perseverance*', TED, 2013, www.ted.com/talks/angela_lee_duckworth_grit_the_power_of_passion_and_perseverance, accessed 25 September 2023

Dunning, D, 'Why incompetent people think they're amazing', TED, 2019, www.ted.com/talks/david_dunning_why_incompetent_people_think_they_re_amazing, accessed 25 September 2023

Dweck, C, Mindset - *Updated Edition: Changing The Way You think To Fulfil Your Potential*, Robinson, 2017

Dyck, A, Morse, A, Zingales, L, 'How pervasive is corporate fraud?', *Review of Accounting Studies*, 2023

Eurich, T, 'What Self-Awareness Really Is (and How to Cultivate It) – It's not just about introspection', Harvard Business Review, January 2018, https://hbr.org/2018/01/what-self-awareness-really-is-and-how-to-cultivate-it, accessed 25 September 2023

Ferriss, T, *Tools of Titans: The Tactics, Routines, and Habits of Billionaires, Icons, and World-Class Performers*, Houghton Mifflin Harcourt, 2016

Friedman, M, 'A Friedman Doctrine: The Social Responsibility of Business is to Increase Its Profits', *The New York Times Magazine*, 13 September 1970

Gallup, 'State of the Global Workplace: 2021 Report', Gallup, 2021, www.gallup.com/workplace/349484/state-of-the-global-workplace.aspx, accessed 25 September 2023

Gawande, A, 'Want to get great at something? Get a coach', TED, 2017, www.ted.com/talks/atul_gawande_want_to_get_great_at_something_get_a_coach, accessed 25 September 2023

Gilbert, DT, *Stumbling on Happiness*, NY: Vintage Books, 2007

Gladwell, M, *Outliers: The Story of Success*, Penguin, 2009

Goleman, D, *Emotional Intelligence: Why It Can Matter More than IQ*, NY: Bantam Books, 1995

Griffin, A, 'Three Words You Need for Your Next Hard Conversation', Medium, 10 August 2020, https://forge.medium.com/three-words-you-need-for-your-next-hard-conversation-a3e2090d043d, accessed 25 September 2023

Gross, B, 'The single biggest reason why start-ups succeed', TED, 2015, www.ted.com/talks/bill_gross_the_single_biggest_reason_why_start_ups_succeed, accessed 25 September 2023

Henderlong, J, Lepper, MR, 'The Effects of Praise on Children's Intrinsic Motivation: A Review and Synthesis', *Psychological Bulletin*, 128(5), 774–795, https://doi.org/10.1037/0033-2909.128.5.774, accessed 25 September 2023

Hunt et al., 'Why Diversity Matters', McKinsey & Company, 2015, www.mckinsey.com/capabilities/people-and-organizational-performance/our-insights/why-diversity-matters, accessed 25 September 2023

Kahneman, K, Deaton, A, 'High Income Improves Evaluation of Life But Not Emotional Well-Being', *Proceedings of the National Academy of Sciences*, 107(38), September 2010, https://doi.org/10.1073/pnas.1011492107, accessed 25 September 2023

Laloux, F, *Reinventing Organizations: A guide to creating organizations inspired by the next stage of human consciousness*, Nelson Parker, 2014

Layard, R, 'Good Jobs and Bad Jobs', CEP *Occasional Paper No 19*, London School of Economics, 2004, https://eprints.lse.ac.uk/28757/1/OP019.pdf, accessed 25 September 2023

Lencioni, P, *The Five Dysfunctions of a Team: A Leadership Fable*, John Wiley & Sons, 2002

Levine et al., 'Accuracy and artifact: Reexamining the intensity bias in affective forecasting', *Journal of Personality and Social Psychology,* 103(4), 2012, 584–605, https://doi.org/10.1037/a0029544, accessed 25 September 2023

Lipton, V, 'A Startling 98% Of Managers Feel Managers Need More Training', Forbes, 2016, https://www.forbes.com/sites/victorlipman/2016/10/01/a-startling-98-of-managers-feel-managers-need-more-training/?sh=776693b5e8bf, accessed 25 September 2023

Livingston et al., 'Nice Guys Finish Last', Kellogg School of Management, 2011, https://insight.kellogg.northwestern.edu/article/nice_guys_finish_last, accessed 25 September 2023

Lublin, JS, 'Job Candidates Get a Manual From Boss: "How to Handle Me"', T*he Wall Street Journal*, 2003, www.wsj.com/articles/SB1041881615563021064, accessed 25 September 2023

Morieux, Y, 'As work gets more complex, 6 rules to simplify', TED, 2014, www.ted.com/talks/yves_morieux_as_work_gets_more_complex_6_rules_to_simplify, accessed 25 September 2023

Nink, M, 'Many Employees Don't Know What's Expected of Them at Work', *Gallup Business Journal,* 2015, https://news.gallup.com/businessjournal/186164/employees-don-know-expected-work.aspx, accessed 25 September 2023

Norton, M, 'How to buy happiness', TED, 2012, www.ted.com/talks/michael_norton_how_to_buy_happiness, accessed 25 September 2023

Pink, DH, 'The Flip Manifesto', 2013, www.danpink.com/wp-content/uploads/2013/07/FLIP-Manifesto.pdf, accessed 25 September 2023

Riggs, K, Riggs, R, *Counter Mentor Leadership: How to Unlock the Potential of the 4-Generation Workplace*, Nicholas Brealey Publishing, 2018

Robert Walters, 'The role of workplace culture in recruiting top talent', Robert Walters, 2019, www.robertwaltersgroup.com/content/dam/robert-walters/country/united-kingdom/files/whitepapers/Robert-Walters-Cultural-Fit-Whitepaper.pdf, accessed 25 September 2023

Schneyer, F, '58% of Managers Never got Supervisor Training', PLANSPONSOR, 2011, www.plansponsor.com/58-of-managers-never-got-supervisor-training, accessed 25 September 2023

Schulman, P, 'Applying Learned Optimism to Increase Sales Productivity', *Journal of Personal Selling and Sales Management* 19(1), October 2013

Seligman et al., 'The Attributional Style Questionnaire', *Cognitive Therapy and Research* 6(3):287-299, January 1982

Seligman ME, 'Learned helplessness', Annual Review of Medicine 23 (1): 407–412, 1972, https://doi.org/10.1146/annurev.me.23.020172.002203, accessed 25 September 2023

Semler, R, 'Managing Without Managers', *Harvard Business Review*, 1989

Sinek, S, *The Infinite Game: How Great Businesses Achieve Long-Lasting Success,* Portfolio Penguin, 2019

Smith, A, *The theory of moral sentiments,* 1759

Stewart, H, 'The Happy Manifesto', Happy, 2012, www.happy.co.uk/media/1910/happy-manifesto-2019.pdf, accessed 25 September 2023

Sutton, RI, *The No Asshole Rule: Building a Civilized Workplace and Surviving One That Isn't*, Business Plus, 2007

Syed, M, *Rebel ideas: The Power of Diverse Thinking*, John Murray, 2020

Tenbrunsel, A, Messick, DM, *'Ethical Fading: The Role of Self-Deception in Unethical Behavior'*, Social Justice Research 17(2):223-236, January 2004

Terkel, S, Working: *People Talk About What They Do All Day and How They Feel About What They Do*, Pantheon/Random House, 1974

Unilever, 'Brands with purpose grow – and here's the proof', Unilever, 2019, www.unilever.com/news/news-search/2019/brands-with-purpose-grow-and-here-is-the-proof, accessed 25 September 2023

Varotto, A, Spagnolli, A, 'Psychological strategies to promote household recycling. A systematic review with meta-analysis of validated field interventions', Journal of Environmental Psychology, 51, August 2017, 166–168, https://doi.org/10.1016/j.jenvp.2017.03.011, accessed 25 September 2023

Waldinger, R, 'What makes a good life? Lessons from the longest study on happiness', TED, 2015, www.ted.com/talks/robert_waldinger_what_makes_a_good_life_lessons_from_the_longest_study_on_happiness

West, C, *The Karpman Drama Triangle Explained: A Guide for Coaches, Managers, Trainers, Therapists – and Everybody Else*, CWTK Publications, 2020

Widrich, L, 'What We Got Wrong When We Tried Flat Management', Fast Company, 2015, www.fastcompany.com/3050759/what-we-got-wrong-about-holacracy, accessed 25 September 2023

Zes, D, Landis, D, 'A Better Return on Self-Awareness', Korn Ferry, 2013, www.kornferry.com/institute/647-a-better-return-on-self-awareness, accessed 25 September 2023

Printed in Great Britain
by Amazon

48270818R00136